MOUNTAIN WARRIORS

The Stackpole Military History Series

THE AMERICAN CIVIL WAR

Cavalry Raids of the Civil War
Ghost, Thunderbolt, and Wizard
Pickett's Charge
Witness to Gettysburg

WORLD WAR II

Armor Battles of the Waffen-SS, 1943–45
Army of the West
Australian Commandos
The B-24 in China
Backwater War
The Battle of Sicily
Beyond the Beachhead
The Brandenburger Commandos
The Brigade
Bringing the Thunder
Coast Watching in World War II
Colossal Cracks
A Dangerous Assignment
D-Day to Berlin
Dive Bomber!
A Drop Too Many
Eagles of the Third Reich
Exit Rommel
Fist from the Sky
Flying American Combat Aircraft of World War II
Forging the Thunderbolt
Fortress France
The German Defeat in the East, 1944–45
German Order of Battle, Vol. 1
German Order of Battle, Vol. 2
German Order of Battle, Vol. 3
The Germans in Normandy
Germany's Panzer Arm in World War II
GI Ingenuity
The Great Ships
Grenadiers
Infantry Aces
Iron Arm
Iron Knights
Kampfgruppe Peiper at the Battle of the Bulge
Kursk
Luftwaffe Aces
Massacre at Tobruk
Mechanized Juggernaut or Military Anachronism?
Messerschmitts over Sicily
Michael Wittmann, Vol. 1
Michael Wittmann, Vol. 2
Mountain Warriors
The Nazi Rocketeers
On the Canal
Operation Mercury
Packs On!
Panzer Aces
Panzer Aces II
Panzer Commanders of the Western Front
The Panzer Legions
Panzers in Winter
The Path to Blitzkrieg
Retreat to the Reich
Rommel's Desert Commanders
Rommel's Desert War
The Savage Sky
A Soldier in the Cockpit
Soviet Blitzkrieg
Stalin's Keys to Victory
Surviving Bataan and Beyond
T-34 in Action
Tigers in the Mud
The 12th SS, Vol. 1
The 12th SS, Vol. 2
The War against Rommel's Supply Lines
War in the Aegean

THE COLD WAR / VIETNAM

Cyclops in the Jungle
Flying American Combat Aircraft: The Cold War
Here There Are Tigers
Land with No Sun
Street without Joy
Through the Valley

WARS OF THE MIDDLE EAST

Never-Ending Conflict

GENERAL MILITARY HISTORY

Carriers in Combat
Desert Battles
Guerrilla Warfare

MOUNTAIN WARRIORS

Moroccan Goums in World War II

Edward L. Bimberg

STACKPOLE
BOOKS

Published in paperback in 2008 by
STACKPOLE BOOKS
5067 Ritter Road
Mechanicsburg, PA 17055
www.stackpolebooks.com

THE MOROCCAN GOUMS: TRIBAL WARRIORS IN A MODERN WAR, by Edward L. Bimberg, was originally published in hard cover by Praeger, an imprint of Greenwood Publishing Group, Inc., Westport, CT.

Cover design by Tracy Patterson

Printed in the United States of America

10 9 8 7 6 5 4 3 2 1

Library of Congress Cataloging-in-Publication Data:

Bimberg, Edward L., 1919–
[Moroccan goums]
Mountain warriors : Moroccan goums in World War II / Edward L. Bimberg.
p. cm. — (Stackpole military history series)
Originally published under the title: The Moroccan goums. 1999.
Includes bibliographical references and index.
ISBN-13: 978-0-8117-3461-5
ISBN-10: 0-8117-3461-7
1. France. Armée—Colonial forces—Morocco. 2. France—Colonies—Africa—Defenses. 3. World War, 1939–1945—Campaigns—Western Front. 4. Morocco—History, Military. I. Title.
D761.9.M67B56 2008
940.54'1244—dc22

2007043150

Contents

Introduction

Shortly after arriving in Corsica in early January 1944, our antiaircraft artillery battalion found itself encamped on a hillside overlooking the city of Bastia. On the second morning of our bivouac, not long after reveille, we heard a strange chanting sound, growing ever louder. In the distance we saw what looked to us like a circus parade.

Coming up the mountain road was a bizarre caravan led by a mounted French officer. The fact that in this overwhelmingly mechanized war he was riding a horse was peculiar enough, but there was more. While his sky-blue *kepi* was typically French and quite familiar, the rest of his costume was not. For over his uniform he wore a *djellaba,* the rough, homespun cloak of the Moroccan mountaineer, striped in black, brown and white. It contrasted strangely with the business-like pistol, map case and field glasses strapped across these exotic robes, and the military boots not quite concealed beneath them.

Riding directly behind him was his guidon bearer, a bearded, hawk-nosed Moroccan in turban and *djellaba.* Only it wasn't an ordinary guidon he carried, for the staff was topped not by the conventional spearhead device but by a shiny brass crescent of Islam, and flowing from it was a long white horsetail swinging in the breeze. Marching in sandaled feet behind the guidon were about a hundred chanting Moroccan tribesmen, all bearded and steely eyed and wearing striped *djellabas* and black turbans. They were carrying American M1903 Springfield rifles and some were leading lop-eared mules heavily burdened with machine guns and supplies. And many of them carried more personal weapons—vicious-looking knives.

Bringing up the rear of the column was the reconnaissance platoon—a couple of dozen tribesmen mounted on the tough little Barb horses native to Morocco. The whole parade looked like something out of the *Arabian Nights*—one almost expected to see a flying carpet go by in aerial support.

That was our introduction to the Moroccan Goumiers—although we'd been hearing about them since we arrived on the Mediterranean shores six months before. Recruited from the primitive hill tribes of Morocco's Atlas Mountains, the Goumiers eventually fought against the Germans in Tunisia, Sicily, Corsica, Italy, France and Germany and quickly became known for their aggressiveness and ferocity and their particular skill in mountain warfare. In Italy, 12,000 strong, they swarmed over the forbidding Aurunci range (which no one thought could be penetrated by any sizable force) to spearhead the French Expeditionary Corps in turning the German flank in Operation Diadem, the final drive on Rome. Their later exploits in the Vosges Mountains in France and the drive to the Rhine and beyond were equally sensational. They ended the war, triumphant, on the banks of the Danube.

In the next few months in Corsica we came to know the Goumiers and to admire them, but because of their reputation for savagery we were, at first, somewhat nervous around them. They were friendly enough, but there were a few contretemps. Two of our batteries provided the antiaircraft defense for the airfield at Borgo, a few miles south of Bastia, where the Goumiers were on security duty. Relations between the Americans and the Moroccans were fine—in the daytime. At night, however, our people complained that the Goumiers would somehow slip silently past the sentries, wiggle under the tent flaps and raid the barracks bags of the sleeping Americans, taking anything they wanted.

"I don't know how they did it," a sergeant remarked in wonder, "but we never heard a damn thing!"

At our request, however, and luckily before someone was shot, their officers quickly put an end to these typically Berber shenanigans.

Those French officers with whom we fraternized at the Florida Club, the dingy Allied officers' watering hole in Bastia, impressed us with their sheer hatred of the Germans, their burning desire to get out of this Mediterranean sideshow and into the main event in Italy. They were part of the 2nd Group of Moroccan Tabors that had fought in Tunisia and chased the Germans out of Corsica. They had taken their share of casualties, but were incredibly eager to get back in the fray. "We want to kill Germans!" they said. And they meant it.

The opportunity of observing the Goumiers on their home ground came when I was invited to a sort of combined field day and horse show at their encampment near Borgo. It was obviously designed to keep the men busy and relieve the boredom of security duty while they waited for their next fight. The men gave exhibitions of mounted drill and horsemanship, the officers rode in a jumping competition and everyone had a great time. It was all innocent, childish fun. One found it hard to equate these laughing, good natured gamesters with their reputation as savage killers.

That they were "irregulars" there was no doubt. There was an atmosphere of informality about the encampment. You saw no saluting; Goumiers and officers greeted each other with the Muslim gesture of hand to lips and heart. Although most of the French officers wore the same *djellaba* as the men (but with the golden galons of their rank attached), there was considerable variety in the rest of their uniforms. The 2nd GTM had received American arms, but apparently little else. The Frenchmen's *kepis* were somewhat battered, their riding boots and puttees (when they had them) were scuffed and worn. Some wore odds and ends of British battle dress. But also seen was that emblem of Continental authority, the walking stick, and that unmistakable symbol of French nobility, the monocle. In spite of their enforced shabbiness these men had an air about them. They were soldiers and there was no doubt about it.

The Goumiers had made a great reputation for themselves as fighting men, but there were serious problems, too. They had come from a wild, remote land, and their background had been unlike that of most other soldiers. When the French came to Morocco and penetrated its untamed interior, they found a violent people constantly engaged in intertribal warfare, where blood feuds, murder and rape were the natural order of things. By 1934 they had pacified those areas, but only just, and as the conquered tribes surrendered, one by one, they recruited their fiercest warriors into the French irregular forces—the Goums.

With that lurid background it was hardly surprising when disgrace visited the Goums in 1944. For in Italy, at the height of their reputation as the best mountain fighters in the Allied camp, discipline broke down and a number of Goumiers went on a wild spree of looting and rape. Their officers quickly punished the offenders, but the ill repute stuck like battlefield mud, and even Pope Pius XII objected to the use of these "savage Africans" on the European continent. In spite of the pope, however, the Goums were sent on into France, and by the end of the war, the misdeeds of the few had been dimmed by the sacrifices of the many—and by time.

The memories that remained were of perhaps the most effective mountain infantry of World War II—and certainly the most colorful.

Author's Note

In a military narrative that takes place over a number of years and with many characters, it is virtually impossible in all instances to maintain the correct correlation between rank and time. However, every effort has been made to give each officer his correct rank at the time of the action involved.

French military ranks found in the text that American readers might find unfamiliar are:

Aspirant: commissioned officer ranking just below second lieutenant; there is no U.S. equivalent

Adjudant: equals U.S. warrant officer

Moquaddem: equals U.S. sergeant

Maoun: equals U.S. corporal

The unit mentioned as the 1st Motorized Division in Italy had its name changed in France to the 1st Free French Division (1st DFL) for political reasons. It was, however, the same unit with the same commanding officer, Colonel Brosset.

CHAPTER 1

Mountain Snows, Desert Palms, Savage Tribes

Morocco, the farthest west of the Barbary States that stretch across North Africa, is a land of varied terrain and differing cultures. It has both Mediterranean and Atlantic coastlines, but the interior is dominated by the Atlas Mountains that rise to snow-covered peaks as high as 13,000 feet and then slope southward into the desert reaches and oasis towns of the Sahara. From time immemorial right into the twentieth century these mountains were the home of fierce warlike tribes in constant conflict with each other and with whatever central government ruled at the time.

In the early part of this century Morocco was still independent but was coveted by all the major European powers. Great Britain, France, Germany, Spain, Italy—all were caught up in a virtual feeding frenzy of colonialism—and the most sought after dish was Morocco, a primitive country only loosely controlled by a weak native government headed by a sultan and known as the Makhzen.

By 1907 the French already had a strong foothold in the country. It had diplomatic relations with the Makhzen in Fez and commercial interests in the coastal cities and towns. And it was soon to have an all-important military presence—which was essential because many officials in the French government had every intention of having France tale all of Morocco (this was in spite of the opposition of Morocco's numerous warlike tribes, to say nothing of the other European powers).

There had long been anti-European sentiment among Moroccans, and in 1907 it boiled over in Casablanca, the west coast port that was Morocco's most important commercial city. In July of that year eight European construction workers were killed by native rioters in an anti-French demonstration that turned deadly. This was followed by an orgy of looting and killing, which in turn triggered a landing by French sailors from the gunboat *Gallilèe.* When they were unable to control the situation, the gunboat shelled the native quarter of the city, killing hundreds. This in turn caused more rioting, and to protect the Europeans of the area, Georges Clemenceau, the French prime minister, dispatched an expeditionary force of some 2,000 men under General Antoine Drude to the scene.

Predictably, this act caused the disorder to spread throughout the Chaouia, the countryside around Casablanca, with the tribes in open revolt. At first the French government hesitated to send its troops beyond the city limits, fearful of both the savagery of the local tribes and the condemnation of the rival European nations. Eventually, however, Drude's columns were reinforced and spread throughout the Chaouia, crushing the numerically superior tribesmen with their overpowering weaponry, which included machine guns and artillery.

A small part of this French force were two company-size units of local native troops. These irregulars were exclusively cavalry and used for reconnaissance and police duty. Each company was called a "Goum," its individual members "Goumiers." It was not until 1908, however, that four more Goums were recruited under the command of Commandant Henri Simon and each Goum organized more formally into infantry and cavalry platoons with a mule train and a section of machine guns. This, then, was the actual birth of the Moroccan Goums, the irregulars who were to play such a spectacular part in World War II.[1]

In due course and after intense diplomatic maneuvering with Germany, England and Spain, plus an agreement with the sultan, much of the country was occupied by French troops that crossed the Algerian border in 1912 and established a protectorate. From that year on, while nominally ruled by the sultan, Morocco was actually controlled by a French resident-general aided by a staff of French military officers and supported by a French army. This Gallic presence immediately and vigorously set about the task of pacifying that wild, intractable land.

The Grand Old Man of Moroccan pacification was General Louis-Hubert Lyautey, the country's first resident-general. A handsome, dignified soldier with snow white hair and a magnificent flowing moustache, Lyautey had cut his teeth on French colonial policy in Indo-China where he had served under General Joseph Gallieni. Gallieni had governed that French colony by "indirect rule" whereby the local native ruling class did the governing, watched over by a velvet-gloved patriarchal French representative. A sincere idealist, Lyautey was determined to put this same policy into effect in Morocco. He really believed that he was bringing the blessings of French civilization into a benighted land.[2]

His task was exceptionally difficult, however. The sultan's fragile government, the Makhzen, which the French supported, had little influence on the quarreling, belligerent tribal chieftains who were unendingly at war with each other and with the central power. Lyautey tried to settle these differences by political and diplomatic means, but he was only partially successful. He finally came to the conclusion that in dealing with the tribes, diplomacy would have to be backed up by military force.

The general was still determined, however, that much of the force should be exerted by the tribesmen themselves. To this end, more auxiliary fighters were organized from the tribes to reinforce the regular French North African troops, the *Tirailleurs* and *Spahis*, in pacifying the dissidents. The responsibility for this was assigned to the French officers of the *Service Des Affaires Indigènes et Renseignements*, the army's combined native affairs department and intelligence service, who decided that these auxiliaries should be divided into three distinct groups: Partisans, Mokhaznis and Goums.[3]

The Partisans were certain of the tribes themselves currently warring against those rival tribes still resisting the French at that particular time. The Mokhaznis were also friendly tribesmen but were more tightly organized in small bands, partially uniformed by the French and more closely supervised than the Partisans. Although both bodies subsequently did useful work in the service of the French, they were not always considered reliable or trustworthy.

The Goums were different. They were the elite of the auxiliary forces, trained, armed, clothed and equipped by the French army. A Goum was eventually a disciplined company-size unit of Moroccans of anywhere from 100 to 170, generally recruited from the most war-like tribes of the remote mountain regions. They were distinguished from the regular North African infantry in the French service, the Tirailleurs, by both mission and dress. The Tirailleurs were regular native soldiers, uniformed, trained and equipped similarly to other French troops and with the same infantry mission. The Goumiers, on the other hand, were paramilitary police whose primary assignment was to maintain order among the fiercely independent tribes of their own regions—and this often led to some heavy fighting. Their uniform was the traditional striped *djellaba*, the homespun woolen garment of the Moroccan tribesman, worn with a turban and sandals. They were armed with regulation French rifles and bayonets and each Goumier equipped himself with a native *koumia*, a rather nasty looking knife with a long, sharp blade.

But even more important than their police duties, the Goums were regularly attached to the *Groupes Mobiles*, the newly formed pacification troops, as guides and scouts—and frequently formed the leading combat elements of these units. They were particularly useful in this role since they knew their own regions well and were very much at home in the difficult mountain terrain.

The French high command found that there were two main stumbling blocks in the path of pacification. The first of these was the terrain. The Atlas ranges of Morocco were no ordinary mountains, but a series of incredibly rugged peaks and valleys, cliffs, gullies, pinnacles and chasms, in places a veritable moonscape that made military operations virtually impossible for conventional troops.

The second problem was the dissident tribesmen themselves. Unlike the Arabs and Arabized Berbers of the Moroccan towns and lowlands, the mountain people (including those who wintered in the plains and lower valleys) were mainly of pure Berber stock, folk who had survived for centuries in that harsh environment. They were unbelievably tough, fearless and enured to the hardships and cruelties of war. According to their French antagonists, their chief characteristic was a spirit of independence that bordered on downright anarchy and made it impossible for them to see the advantages of a peaceful, orderly existence under the *pax Gallica.* No one who had not fought against them could ever understand what stubborn, wily, dangerous opponents they could be.

The *Groupes Mobiles* were eventually conceived by the French high command to solve these two main problems. Each *Groupe Mobile* varied considerably in composition, custom designed for a particular operation in a specific area, but all had certain similarities. Headed by a senior officer with a small staff, a typical *Groupe Mobile* might consist of several battalions of regular infantry (*Tirailleurs,* or Foreign Legion), a squadron of cavalry (*Spahis*) and a few batteries of field or mountain artillery.[4] In addition—and of major importance—would be a contingent of tribal auxiliaries, the most effective of which were the one or two Goums that usually formed the point and flank guard of the entire expedition. When the terrain became too difficult for the cavalry and where even the regular infantry couldn't penetrate, it was up to the men of the Goums. For the Goumiers, maneuvering around the almost unscalable cliffs and crags and attacking the dissidents in their rocky lair was literally child's play, for they were themselves true mountain Berbers raised as children in just such nightmarish country. Besides, the French native affairs officers who led the Goums had probably supplied much of the intelligence for that particular *Groupe Mobile* and knew exactly what tribes they were fighting, who their leaders were and where their strongholds were located.

These French officers of the *Service des Affaires Indigènes* were more than just soldiers. They were a combination of warrior, social worker, ethnologist and spy who had studied the Berbers of Morocco and knew their charges well, both their own men and the enemy they hoped to convert to friends. But leading the Goumiers was not easy, for the Berbers were a complicated people. The Goumiers themselves represented a variety of customs, tribes and regions. Some were swarthy, others lighter of skin and there was also a sprinkling of Negroid types whose ancestors had wandered into the Atlas regions from the sub-Sahara. The origins of the Berber people are largely unknown. It was thought that there was a mixture of early conquerers—Carthaginian, Roman, Vandal and Byzantine—somewhere in their background, but that's just an educated guess. They had been in Africa long before the Arab conquests of the Middle Ages—some thought as early as 2000 B.C.—and while the Moroccans had succeeded in keeping most of the Arabs out of the mountains, they had adopted their religion and were nominally devout Muslims.[5]

Arabic was the general language of the lowlands and while it was spoken by some of the hill people as well, most of the Atlas tribesmen spoke only Berber. To add to the general confusion there were two distinct dialects—Tamazight and Tashilhit—but no written language. For the French officers linguistic ability was just one more challenge, and although early on they used native interpreters, many became quite facile in the native tongues.

The Goumiers were superb soldiers. Short, bearded men, they were lean and wiry, hard as their rocky surroundings and capable of the most amazing feats of endurance. Neither extreme heat nor frigid cold seemed to bother them, and they remained cheerful no matter what. Their exceptionally keen eyesight[6] made them good marksmen, although in close combat they preferred to use their ever-present knives. Their officers liked and admired them, and they returned the compliment; there was seldom any question of their loyalty and devotion.

Each Goum was usually divided into several sections of infantry and a platoon of cavalry, the latter riding in high-backed Arab saddles on tough little North African Barb horses. A mule train for supplies and a section of Hotchkiss machine guns completed the picture. It was a highly mobile unit perfectly suited to its mission in the roadless highlands of Morocco.

Almost immediately upon taking office as resident-general in 1912, Lyautey was faced with a series of military and diplomatic emergencies. In Fez itself, the Seat of government, there was a revolt, aided by a tribal coalition outside the walls, that had to be put down by force. Then the present sultan, Abd el-Hafid, was not cooperating in a manner that satisfied the resident-general, so Lyautey, working behind the scenes, encouraged his abdication and replaced him with a more compliant ruler, Moulay Youseff. This caused great concern throughout the tribes and a pretender appeared, one Ahmed el-Hiba, who declared himself sultan with headquarters in Marrakesh, principal city of the south. It was learned, moreover, that he was holding eight Europeans as prisoners in that ancient town. This, of course, would never do, so Lyautey summoned his toughest general, Charles Mangin,[7] and ordered him to Marrakesh to rescue the captives and get rid of el-Hiba.

The veteran Mangin was delighted with the order and set off for Marrakesh with 5,000 men. Everywhere he met overwhelming numbers of hostile tribesmen—and everywhere he defeated them, again thanks largely to his automatic weapons and artillery. Even before reaching Marrakesh, the French had inflicted hundreds of casualties on their opponents at a cost to themselves of only two dead and twenty-three wounded. The worst that the bulk of the Mangin column suffered was exhaustion, and the general called a halt just short of his goal to give his men and animals a rest. However, he sent an advance column under Commandant Simon, his second in command and the man who had organized the first Goums in the Chaouia, into Marrakesh where the captives were rescued alive and unhurt. El-Hiba and his followers had fled, headed for the High Atlas where the French were hesitant to follow.

The Atlas Mountains were a difficult challenge for Lyautey. He knew that to rule Morocco he must conquer those forbidding highlands, but he was not yet ready. Not only were the peaks and valleys terrain that made military operations extremely difficult, but the tribes of the mountains were even tougher and more belligerent than those of the plains. To make matters even more difficult for Lyautey, some of his colonels in the field were getting a bit out of hand, going further in their pursuit of rebellious tribesmen than the resident-general desired. He didn't want the French iron hand showing through a tattered velvet glove, but that was the way it was beginning to look.

General Mangin was the worst offender. After Marrakesh he established posts along the right bank of the Oum er Rebia, the river that was the extreme border of French penetration and beyond which Lyautey had forbidden any of his soldiers to go. When the post at Kasbah Tadla was attacked by tribesmen under Moha ou Said, a well-known and respected leader in that region and long an enemy of the French, Mangin thought it was time to cross the river and punish the raiders. Simon, now, in 1914, a colonel and head of French intelligence, agreed. Lyautey somewhat reluctantly gave his permission, but

Wearing a French helmet and a traditional *djellaba,* a goumier sharpens his bayonet in Sicily, 1943. NATIONAL ARCHIVES

demanded that Mangin first try to settle their differences with Moha ou Said by negotiation. The fiery Mangin and the more sensible Simon then entered into talks with the Berber war chief, but to no avail; Moha ou Said was just as hard-nosed as Mangin and the parley went nowhere. The result was that Mangin took a strong force across the Oum er Ribia and struck hard at the tribesmen's base camp at El Ksiba.

The battle at El Ksiba lasted for two days, and if one kept score by numbers of killed and wounded, the French won hands down. But Mangin's people also took heavy casualties—more than 60 dead and 150 wounded—and marched back to

Kasbah Tadla harried by snipers and leaving a significant amount of equipment scattered along the way. And Moha ou Said made his escape to fight another day. Lyautey was satisfied simply to reinforce Kasbah Tadla and the posts along the right side of the river and to try to quiet the tribes on the other side of the river by political means. He had things on his mind other than the Tadla region.

By 1914 Lyautey was ready to start spreading French influence further into the Middle Atlas, hopefully by political means, but if necessary by force of arms. Standing in his way was a man named Moha ou Hammou, leader of the Zaïan confederation of belligerent Berber tribes who roamed in the region of the holy city of Khenifra near the foothills of the Atlas. These people were considered mountain tribes, for although they came down with their flocks to the plains and lower valleys when the winters became too harsh, they were allied with some of the toughest mountain people who had sworn eternal enmity to the French. To make matters more difficult for Lyautey, Moha ou Said, who had escaped from Mangin at Ksiba, was back in the picture and had now formed an entente with Moha ou Hammou. Another Berber chieftain, the powerful religious leader Ali Amhaouch, known as "the sultan of the mountains" became the third member of this formidable triumvirate.

Finally realizing that "political action" would have no effect on these determined hill people, Lyautey authorized Colonel Paul Henrÿs, one of his more astute officers as far as knowledge of the tribes was concerned, to take command of all French forces in the field, defeat the tribes of the Zaïan confederation in battle and occupy their headquarters city of Khenifra.

On June 10, 1914, Henrÿs sent three separate columns marching against Khenifra, one from the Meknès region under Lieutenant-Colonel Henri Claudel, another from Rabat commanded by Lieutenant-Colonel Guillaume Cros and the third from the Tadla area under Colonel Noël Garnier-Duplessis.

This combined force of 14,000 men with every modern weapon of war, including accompanying reconnaissance planes, also included a considerable force of Goumiers. The French had found the Goums increasingly valuable, particularly as the terrain became ever more rugged, and by 1914 there were no fewer than fifteen Goums[8] in the French service.

Two of the columns descending on Khenifra met with little resistance, but the Claudel column suffered constant attack almost from the start. The French, however, held their own, and on June 12 caught Moha ou Hammou by surprise, dispersing his tribesmen with artillery fire. For a while Claudel met no more opposition, but as he neared Khenifra and joined the other two columns, the combined force came under heavy attack from the mountains. In spite of the ferocity of the attack and the traditional Berber disregard for danger and contempt for death, the assault was beaten off with few French losses and the pacification forces entered Khenifra. It was empty, as was the countryside around it. The tribesmen had disappeared into the mountains.

While this appeared a triumph for French arms, it was a disappointment to Henrÿs, for now there was no one with whom to parley, and the "political" side of Lyautey's pacification theory was left hanging in midair. Nor was the military side over with, for Moha was soon back, attacking the French camp at Khenifra. Once again the attack was beaten off with heavy Berber losses, and once again Moha retreated into the mountains. But Moha ou Hammou was nothing if not persistent. He continued to harass the French presence around Khenifra, and while he took tremendous losses he always seemed to bounce back. And as powerful as the French proved themselves to be, Moha still maintained his prestige and leadership among the tribes.

Now Henrÿs decided to prop up the French defenses throughout the combat zone. He strengthened the borderline along the Oum er Rebia by posting a *Groupe Mobile* of four battalions under Lieutenant-Colonel René Laverdure at Khenifra, with two other *Groupes* to the east and west under Claudel and Garnier-Duplessis respectively. He then established two new posts at Mriret and Sidi Lamine, and put his Goums to work patrolling in between, to protect the territory from roving bands of pillaging Berbers.

Even so, the attacks continued. To make matters worse, the "guns of August" began to roar; World War I had started and thirty-seven French battalions were withdrawn from Morocco to fight in Europe.[9] This further encouraged the Berbers to increase their attacks throughout Morocco, a movement additionally inspired by the infiltration of German agents into the protectorate, promising all sorts of clandestine military support. During this time Khenifra suffered continuous assault, but the defenses of the city held. Then, toward the end of August, the *Groupes Mobiles* of Garnier-Duplessis and Claudel fell upon the separate bands of Moha ou Hammou and Ali Amhaouch inflicting stinging defeats on both. In September the troops that had been sent to Europe had been replaced by newly raised levies, and things quieted down in the Khenifra area as winter brought more tribes into submission to the French. All seemed calm.

Then in November, French arms received a terrible—and totally unnecessary—setback. Colonel Laverdure, commanding at Khenifra, decided on his own to attack the winter encampment of Moha ou Hammou some eight miles away at El Herri on the left bank of the Oum er Rebia. He had previously proposed this attack to his superiors, but had been turned down. Lyautey still hoped to talk the wily Moha into submission, and the present calm suited French interests. Moreover, in the judgement of the high command, Lavendure did not have sufficient military means to insure success. No matter. On November 13 the glory-hunting Laverdure set out with almost the entire garrison of Khenifra, six companies of Algerian and Senegalese Tirailleurs, two field artillery pieces, a squadron of cavalry and a party of Goumiers. He didn't bother to notify his superiors, Lyautey in Rabat or Henrÿs in Fez, of his action. The move was totally unauthorized.

Laverdure caught Moha completely by surprise. The first knowledge the Berbers had of an attack was the artillery shells exploding amongst their tents, causing destruction and panic. The second phase was a cavalry charge into the wreckage that sent the survivors streaking for the mountains. Moha, as usual, got away, but two of his wives were captured. The French forces then sacked the encampment, taking anything of value that was left behind. As the Laverdure column started back for Khenifra, the tribesmen, who until now had been Moha's allies, came down from the hills and continued the looting of his wrecked camp. They figured that Moha was finished, and they were now on their own, free to seek new alliances.

However, the battle was not yet over. As the French marched home they were attacked by small bands of tribesmen, which they fought off. But more kept coming. And then, as they saw that the French forces were not as strong as they originally thought, even more tribesmen joined the fray. As the word got out, thousands of angry and aroused Berbers poured down from the mountains and enveloped Laverdure's troops. Before the smoke cleared, the fight had turned into a massacre. More than 600 soldiers, including Laverdure and most of his officers, were killed. Only a handful managed to straggle back to the comparative safety of Khenifra, and they wouldn't have made it if the pursuing tribesmen hadn't stopped to loot the bodies of the dead.

Captain Pierre Croll, now in charge of what was left of the Khenifra garrison, immediately telegraphed word of the disaster to Lyautey and Henrÿs—the first they heard of Laverdure's adventure. Henrÿs acted at once, dispatching Garnier-Duplessis'

Groupe Mobile to Khenifra, as well as ordering another *Groupe* to be formed under Lieutenant-Colonel Joseph Dérigoin. By the end of November there were 7,000 French troops defending Khenifra.

Moha ou Hammou, as usual, landed on his feet. After suffering the annihilation of his camp and fleeing into the mountains, he again demonstrated his power and charisma among the tribes by displaying the booty of the Laverdure massacre, the large amounts of captured weaponry. In spite of winter snows and the increased French presence, the dissidence of the Zaïan tribes continued. Sporadic fighting went on throughout 1916 and although the tribesmen always got the worst of it, there was no lessening of their hostility. But even so, more tribes submitted and each submission recruited more warriors for the Goums. By 1917 there were twenty-one Goums in the French service and their reputation as loyal fighting men was secure. They liked soldiering (of the irregular sort) and they liked being on the winning side even more.

While Lyautey had long realized that to break the Zaïan confederation he would have to conquer the peaks of the Middle Atlas, he had heretofore only ventured into the lower reaches of there formidable mountains. In November 1916 he decided it was time. He appointed Colonel Joseph Poeymireau, who had been Henrÿs' second-in-command at Meknès (Henrÿs had requested transfer to the front in France), to take charge of this mission. It was to be a sort of pincer movement, crossing the Atlas from opposite directions with one *Groupe Mobile* under Poeymireau leaving from Meknès, and another under Colonel Paul Doury with its starting point at Bou Denib on the eastern side of the mountains near the Algerian border. They were to join up on the Moulaya River, crushing the dissident tribes between them.

While other mobile groups kept the hostile tribes busy, Poeymireau and Doury accomplished their mission more easily than had been expected. In June 1917 the two trans-Atlas groups met along the Moulaya and a new era of Moroccan pacification had begun.

These paths that opened military traffic through the previously impenetrable mountains marked the beginning of the end for the independence of the Zaïan tribes. Now Lyautey felt he could proceed with the development of central Morocco to the benefit of all. Although there were still hostile tribes and considerable fighting ahead, many new posts and settlements were opened up and some degree of peace settled on the Middle Atlas. To cap this optimistic outlook, in the spring of 1918 the news came out of the mountains that Ali Amhaouch, one of the three prominent hostile leaders, had died of natural causes.

But now there was an uprising in another part of Morocco, the Tafilalet, the eastern section on the other side of the mountains where the Atlas gradually slopes down to the sands and palm trees of the desert oases. Colonel Doury marched his *Groupe Mobile* back down to Gaouz, and after a fierce battle with the rebels, declared victory. But the "victory" cost him the loss of 200 of his own men, to say nothing of horses, mules and equipment. Lyautey was not pleased. He considered the Tafilalet a sideshow that detracted men and material from the main event, which was the pacification of the more northerly regions, "*Maroc utile*," the useful Morocco with an economic future, not the desert wastes near the Algerian border. He thought Doury's action unnecessary, too much like Lavendure's adventure at El Herri. To correct the mistake, Lyautey put Poeymireau in charge in the Tafilalet.

However, as so many military commanders throughout history have discovered, getting in is often much easier than getting out. Poeymireau fought the rebels with everything he could muster—planes, artillery, infantry, cavalry—and finally, having subdued the rebellious tribesmen, returned to Meknès.

He had hardly left when the Tafilalet blew up again. This time Poeymireau returned with reinforcements and fought a series of battles until he was wounded by the accidental explosion of an artillery shell. Colonel Antoine Huré finally finished the job in January 1919, and a degree of calm returned to the Tafilalet—at least for the time being.

The troubles in the Tafilalet were reflected briefly in another flurry of resistance on the other side of the mountains, but this was soon put down. It seemed that at last the Zaïan bloc was beginning to break up. Beginning in 1917 the three sons of Moha ou Hammou held talks with the French, and by 1920 they had become loyal followers of Lyautey and the Makhzen—but their father remained an implacable enemy. The *Groupes Mobiles* kept patrolling through the unsettled areas, with the result that more and more of the hostile tribes finally submitted. Then in 1921 Moha ou Hammou was killed in a skirmish, not with the French, but between two Zaïan tribes. This was the signal for Poeymireau to move against the last of the unconquered Zaïan territory, a mountainous stronghold known as the Bekrit Massif. Three separate *Groupes Mobiles* closed in on the recalcitrant tribesmen, and by 1922 the Zaïan phase of Morocco's pacification was virtually over.

But the third member of that troublesome alliance of Berber leaders, Moha ou Said, was still on the loose. A *Groupe Mobile* under Colonel Henri Fredenburg was sent after him, and after defeating several of his tribes, occupied a number of locations south of the Oum er Rebia, including El Ksiba, the site of Mangin's long ago battle. Once again, however, the defiant and slippery Moha ou Said escaped. Pursued by determined French forces, he fought on in the peaks and valleys of the Middle Atlas, and then fled to the even more rugged fastnesses of the High Atlas. Here his luck gave out; Moha ou Said was killed in a battle with the French in 1924. Many of his followers, however, kept up a guerrilla war against their conquerors throughout the next decade.

In southern Morocco, in the western High Atlas and below Marrakesh, Lyautey operated in a different way. Here he had a chance to put his theory of "indirect rule" to work, using the local *caïds,* the representatives of the Makhzen, to maintain order and perform the other functions of government. In this he was only partially successful. While the Berber partisan tribes did most of the fighting against the dissidents, on at least one occasion the French had to send a column of troops south from Marrakesh to back them up. And of course the French officers of native affairs and the intelligence services (virtually the same thing), those same officers so prominent in the training and command of the Goums, were always on the scene, influencing, supporting and sometimes commanding the local chieftains loyal to the French. The latter were never quite trusted, but the system was pure Lyautey and saved French lives.

The greatest challenge to French rule in Morocco, however, came not from the south, but from the extreme north in the Spanish-ruled territories close to the Mediterranean. Much of this land was a wild, mountainous region known as the Rif, and in 1921 a new and charismatic Berber leader appeared there. His name was Mohammed ben Abd el-Krim el Kellabi and he was quite different from the average Berber chieftain. Abd el-Krim was an educated, sophisticated, well-traveled man who had studied law in Fez, and although he had no formal military training, he seemed to have a natural instinct for combat and in-born qualities of leadership. Combined with his visceral hatred of the Spanish, this made him a dangerous opponent indeed. In July 1921, at the head of an army of Riffian tribesmen, he defeated a strong Spanish garrison at Anual, not far from the Mediterranean coast. This battle was no small feat; it ended with 8,000 Spanish dead, 5,000 wounded and 200 taken prisoner.[10] The Riffians also captured much military hardware, including a large number of artillery pieces, which boded ill for their enemies in future warfare. It was a particularly sweet victory to Abd el-Krim, for the commander of the Spanish troops was General Manuel Silvestre who had previously thrown the Riffian chieftain in jail for some minor offense. He had escaped, gone back to the Rif and raised his own army of rebels. Silvestre had been killed (or committed suicide) in the battle.

It was not too difficult to recruit an army against the Spanish. The Riffians were not only imbued with that typical Berber spirit of independence, but they had very good reason to hate their colonial rulers. The Spanish were cruel, corrupt and incredibly inept at colonial government, and their army was poorly trained and lacking in morale. Krim took advantage of this to push on past Anual almost to the gates of Melilla, the tribesmen murdering, raping and torturing all the way. But the Riffian chieftain stopped his men short of the port city; he knew that if they sacked heavily populated Melilla, every European colonial nation would be against him. Instead, he sent his people marching back to the Rif to reorganize and plan for bigger things.

And bigger things were to come. When Abd el-Krim came down from his native mountains again, he had an even larger and more enthusiastic army with him. An astute politician, he was able to convince more and more of the tribes to join him in his cause, which was primarily to kick the Spanish out of Morocco. (He had other things on his mind, but that would come later.) The Riffians swept across Spanish Morocco, and with every victory they captured more Spanish arms and gained more manpower as the captured tribes joined the Riffian armies. And those that refused to join suffered, for the Riffians proved to be even more brutal than other Berbers, and torture and massacre went hand-in-hand with combat.

At first the uprising in Spanish Morocco did not worry Lyautey too much. He felt it was directed solely at Spanish misrule and had nothing to do with the French. Besides, there was considerable colonial rivalry between the two nations and the resident-general was not too displeased at the Spanish military discomfort. He had no intention of going to the aid of Spain and becoming entangled in even more warfare when his own Middle Atlas problems remained unsettled.

But then the Riffians extended their depredations south of the border with French Morocco. Although the tribes in that region lived in the French zone, many of them had never submitted to the French, and fell willingly under the spell of Abd el-Krim. In addition, his cause had attracted a number of outsiders, including several Europeans among whom was a German adventurer, a deserter from the French Foreign Legion named Joseph Klems.[11] An experienced soldier, Klems was accepted by Abd el-Krim as a military expert and was, indeed, successful in training the Riffians in the use of their captured weapons.

By this time the Riffian revolt was no longer a mere tribal uprising but rather a full-blown holy war, a *jihad* against all colonialism in North Africa, and Lyautey was at last forced to recognize it as such. His first act of recognition was to order the *Groupe Mobile* of Colonel Paul Colombat at Ouezanne to patrol along the border as a show of force to the local tribes and a threat to the Riffian bands invading French territory. From then on things turned from bad to worse for the French. Abd el-Krim became more bold and more powerful, even appealing to the League of Nations for recognition of a Rif Nation.

In Europe and America the revolt became front page news, and sympathy for the Riffian cause grew. An American reporter, Vincent Sheean, managed to find his way to Riffian headquarters and interviewed Abd el-Krim. He painted the rebel leader as a freedom fighter, and the report travelled throughout the world. Even the Foreign Legion deserter, Klems, was romanticized. A Broadway musical called *Desert Song* was supposedly based on the adventures of the German ex-Legionnaire. One of its songs, a rousing ballad called "Rifs!" became popular with theatergoers and radio listeners across America.

Soon the French were forced to formally ally themselves with the Spaniards in fighting the ever more successful tribesmen. More French mobile groups were put in the field, and when it became obvious that Abd el-Krim had his eyes on Fez itself, a defensive line of posts was established north of that important city. When some of those posts had to be abandoned to the enemy, even Lyautey had to admit that the French were losing the battle. There were several French successes, however—hard blows against Riffian bands by *Groupes Mobiles* under Colonel Auguste Noguès and Colonel Columbat—but in spite of these victories, by 1925 the situation had become desperate.

The turnabout in French fortunes came only with the arrival in Morocco of General Henri-Philippe Pétain, the hero of World War I. He had the backing of the French government, the cooperation of Spain and heavy troop reinforcements. As Pétain took full military control in Morocco, it became obvious that Lyautey's star was waning. At age seventy-one, the resident-general, realizing that his role in Morocco was over, resigned and returned to France. Pétain fought on and defeated Abd el-Krim, who surrendered to the French in 1926.

The Rif war had a profound affect on French colonial policy. The casualty lists shocked the folks back home and rocked the politicians in Paris, as well as causing an international uproar against French colonialism. Henceforth the government would have to soft-pedal its operations against the tribes. During the war the Goums had their hands full, for with the main body of regular troops concentrated in the north, they were responsible for security in much of the rest of the protectorate. The troubles in the Rif had stirred up the tribes in all the mountain regions and the Goumiers were kept busy stamping out the simmering fires of rebellion that had started up with the news from the Rif.

During all these turbulent years the Goums remained steadfast. While the tribes of their origin vacillated—loyal to the French one day, fighting them the next—the Goumiers remained faithful, not to France, but to their officers, the

Frenchmen to whom they owed their fealty. Whether the Goums were fighting alongside the regulars in the *Groupes Mobiles* or policing their own mountains, it proved an unbreakable bond. The French always knew they could rely on their tough mountain irregulars, and as the high command realized the value of the Goumiers in the work of pacification, the number of Goums was gradually increased. By the end of the Rif war there were twenty-seven Goums operating throughout the protectorate.

Although the Riffian troubles had shaken the French authorities, by the late 1920s and early 1930s they were beginning to feel that they again had some control. There were still dissident tribes throughout Morocco, but both the size and composition of the *Groupes Mobiles* had changed and the techniques of pacification had been perfected. French columns now roamed throughout Morocco from the northern border to the Tafilalet and along the Draa and Dades rivers to the south, forcing the submission of almost the last of the rebellious tribesmen. As more and more tribes surrendered, French army engineers and the Foreign Legion[12] moved into their territories, building roads, bridges, tunnels and other public works as well as the fortified posts necessary for their continued security. And connecting them all were miles and miles of utility poles and wires. All the while the remaining few dissident tribes were being slowly pushed further into the wilds of the High Atlas.

As the native troops and their French officers penetrated ever more deeply into the barely explored wastes of the southern mountains, the last of the unconquered tribesmen resisted with a savagery that impressed even their tough, battle-tested opponents. The terrain was as rugged as any the French forces had ever seen—sheer mountain walls split by deep narrow canyons with unscalable cliffs from which the tribesmen could deliver a devastating fire.

The French command in these last of the tribal battles in Morocco threw everything they had against the desperate stand of the mountaineers. Typical of this fighting was the attack on the very last holdouts, some 10,000 tribesmen ensconced in the fastnesses of the 12,000-foot-high Mount Baddou. The Berbers had made fortresses of the huge caverns and deep gorges in these terrifying heights and were occupying them with their families and herds. They had blocked the entrances with boulders and it seemed virtually impossible to winkle them out.[13]

The mountain peaks were surrounded by four mobile groups, each the size of a division, the *Groupe du Tadla*, led by General de Loustal, the *Groupe de Meknes* under General Goudot, the *Groupe de Marrakesh* under General Catroux and General Giraud's command, the *Groupe de Confines*, the latter originating on the Algerian border. All these groups were composed of infantry, cavalry, artillery and engineers and by this time all the *Groupes Mobiles* in Morocco had their own aircraft for reconnaissance and bombing. General Giraud's unit even had a few tanks and armored cars, their limited usefulness made possible by the road-building of the engineers and the Legion. There were now forty-eight Goums in Morocco, no less than twenty-five of them in the forces besieging Mount Baddou.[14]

It seems impossible that the Berbers with their archaic arms could hold out against this formidable army with all its modern equipment, but they did. The artillery couldn't reach them in their impenetrable caves, and the airplanes with their bombings couldn't do much damage either, although sometimes the concussion brought down the cavern roofs on the trapped inhabitants. It was also extremely dangerous to fly amongst these peaks and ridges where unpredictable thermal updrafts made control of the aircraft particularly difficult. Finally it was up to the Tirailleurs and Goumiers to crawl up to the cave openings and lob in grenades, a not very profitable undertaking, with many casualties.

Eventually, it was nature that defeated the tribesmen. The French dammed the streams that ran through the Berber positions, cutting off their water supply. Parties of tribesmen had to slip out at night to try to find enough water for their people and animals, a difficult, dangerous and not very successful operation. Not only did they suffer severe casualties doing this, but they could never discover a large enough water supply to make a difference. Finally their suffering proved too much—even for Berbers. Rather than see their families die slowly from thirst, the tribesmen surrendered. In 1933 the last of the dissident tribes, the Aït Abdi, the Aït Sokhlman and, toughest of them all, the Aït Haddidou, came down out of their mountain strongholds and submitted to the French generals. The pacification of Morocco was complete.

This last phase of the French conquest was the strangest part of a strange war. While more than 30,000 French-led troops were engaged in deadly combat, the rest of the world seemed unaware of it. Tourists flocked to the vacation spots of the north with little knowledge of the bloodshed in the south. The French government had learned the lesson of the Rif war; keep the conflict secret and there would be fewer complaints at home and abroad.

From the early 1920s on, the name of one French officer had become particularly associated with the Goums. It was that of Augustin-Léon Guillaume. A short, solidly built man with a prominent nose, piercing eyes under bushy brows, and a thin military moustache, Guillaume was a true *beau sabreur*, by 1941 a hardened veteran of the colonial wars. He was by nature and experience tough, professional and self-confident, a fighter. As a native of the Haute-Alpes region of France he was also a born mountain man, right at home in the rugged hill country of Morocco.

Guillaume's military career hadn't started on a particularly high note. He had graduated from the St. Cyr military academy in 1914 and was almost immediately thrown into the front lines in World War I. Within three months he was a prisoner-of-war and spent the rest of the conflict in German prison camps. He could hardly be blamed for hating *les Boches* ever since.

Upon his release in 1919 he was posted to Morocco, still a wild and turbulent land with a people unhappy under French occupation. In 1921 he was given his first command of irregular Moroccan troops, the 12th Goum of Berber tribesman, and later commanded the 15th Goum. After two years' service with the Goums in that bitter time of heavy fighting, Guillaume knew he had found his niche.

Captain Guillaume missed much of the drama of the Rif war, however, for in 1924 he was sent back to France to continue the climb up the ladder of promotion expected of every promising officer. Along the way he served as a regimental officer in the regular infantry, a staff officer in the French army of occupation in Germany, and after that was adjutant to the French military attaché in Belgrade. Finally he was appointed to the *Ecole Supériore de Guerre*, the war college attended by those officers destined to obtain important commands in the French army.

In the latter part of 1928, Guillaume returned to his beloved Morocco. In the ensuing years he served in a variety of major staff and command jobs, mostly in intelligence and native affairs, including a tour of duty as commander of an entire military area near Marrakesh, the *Cercle d'Azilal.* He kept in close contact with his Goumiers, always an important part of his command, for whom he had formed a special attachment. By 1934 there were fifty-one Goums and Colonel Guillaume, among his other duties, supervised them all.[15]

This was also the time when the machinations of Adolf Hitler brought the hint of a coming war to Europe, and that atmosphere was reflected in the military preparations in Morocco. Guillaume knew that if war came to the Continent, North Africa would be stripped of most of its regular formations, and the Goums would be left to play an increasingly important part in the security of the protectorate. In 1936 Guillaume was made director of Political Affairs in Rabat, the capital, and from that seat of power he would be able to expedite his plans for an increase in the size and training of those irregular forces under his command.

When war finally came in 1939 the magnificent North African regiments of Tirailleurs, Spahis, Zouaves and Chasseurs d'Afrique were, as predicted, sent off to Europe to eventually be ground to pieces in Hitler's blitzkrieg of 1940. Just before that, in May, the first Goums to be engaged in World War II were formed into the *1st Groupe de Supplétifs Marocains* ("supplétifs" is a military term for "auxiliaries"). They were then sent across Algeria to southern Tunisia where they skirmished along the Libyan border with Italian troops, but fought no serious battles. The surrender of the French forces in Europe and the subsequent armistice agreements ended that adventure, and in September the Goums returned to Morocco and were dispersed to their various garrisons, disappointed but not defeated. Soon the remnants of some of the regular units that had fought in France also returned, bloodied, battered and torn, to become part of the new Vichy government's XIX Army Corps in North Africa.

It was a difficult time, but Guillaume knew what he must do. He had not given up hope, and like many other French officers he was already thinking of *revanche*—and the part his Goumiers could play in redeeming the honor of the French army. It would not be easy. Already German and Italian armistice commissioners were in Morocco to see that the armistice agreements were properly carried out. By the terms of the agreements the French were allowed to keep only a certain number of men under arms (120,000 in North Africa) and much of their equipment was to be turned over to the commission or destroyed. According to the French authorities, however, the Goums could not be counted as soldiers but rather as police, for they were carried on the budget of the protectorate as such and charged with the duty of maintaining order among the tribes, and preventing gun-running in the frontier regions. The Axis commissioners, somewhat naively it would seem, agreed.

But Guillaume had other plans for the Goums. Long before the enemy inspectors arrived, he and the other authorities had contrived to hide the weapons forbidden by the commission where they could not be found, deep in the furthest reaches of the Atlas Mountains. Day after day trucks and mule trains loaded with rifles, machine guns, mortars and ammunition made their way along the rough roads and through the valleys and gorges of this forbidding land, to be hidden in the remote valley farms of French settlers or buried among the rocks of the boulder-strewn terrain.

The same charade was going on all over North Africa. When the German and Italian officers arrived, a cat-and-mouse game ensued. The French showed them only what they wanted them to see, and the mountains and deserts of Morocco, Algeria and Tunisia formed far too great an expanse for the inspection teams to explore. Besides, the cafes and bordellos of Casablanca, Algiers and Tunis were far more interesting than the barren wastes of the African bled, and that's what the conquerors preferred to inspect.

The armistice commissioners reported to their superiors in Berlin and Rome that the French army in Africa was indeed thoroughly beaten and presented no threat to Axis ambitions. They were particularly unimpressed by the Goumiers. These dark-skinned little men in their bathrobe-like *djellabas,* turbans and sandals, armed only with rifles and knives, were perhaps useful as back country policemen, but nothing more. The commissioners had seen them on the march, their rifles carried at all sorts of crazy angles, sometimes leading goats (not mascots, but rations on the hoof) and chanting odd Oriental folksongs. It was certainly not the Prussian idea of what disciplined troops should look like, and the thought that these circus clowns would ever be able to stand up as soldiers against the Nazi supermen never entered the Axis' minds. The inspectors treated them with disdain and openly ridiculed their bizarre appearance.

Colonel Guillaume knew better. He had led the Goumiers in action and was aware of their fighting ability. He reasoned that armed with modern weapons, trained diligently and treated with proper respect for their customs and religion, they could become a first class mountain infantry capable of confronting the best the enemy had to offer. He set out to prove it.

The first step was to get authorization for expansion and reorganization. Guillaume was now high enough in the Moroccan military hierarchy for him to be heard, and with the cooperation of Colonel Auguste Noguès,[16] the current resident-general of Morocco, the necessary permission was obtained. Next, secret training areas had to be found, far from the prying eyes of the armistice commission. Considering the remoteness of so much of Morocco, this was not too difficult—and of course the terrain was perfect for training mountain troops. Finally there was the matter of recruiting. The untamed mountaineers of the Atlas had always liked to fight, and service in the Goums had traditionally provided the combat and adventure they so eagerly sought. Now that the word was out that a real big war might be in the offing, many more of the wild Berber tribesmen rushed to join.

To command such enthusiastic but undisciplined warriors required a very special type of officer, and these were carefully chosen. The higher ranking leaders were already there, the veteran native affairs officers who had been lieutenants and captains during the pacification period and were now colonels and higher. As for the junior officers and non-coms (non-commissioned officers), volunteers came from almost every branch of the African army, most of them experienced with native troops. To be successful in the Goums they needed exceptional stamina to keep up with the tough mountain men they were to command plus the mental agility to understand and empathize with the thought processes, customs and traditions of a strange, primitive people. They also needed animal management skills, rare in modern armies, for motor transport was next to useless in the roadless mountains where they expected to fight—it was to be all horses and mules. (These skills were perhaps easier to find among the French forces than in other modern armies, for in spite of the pleadings of a little-known colonel named de Gaulle, the high command had not been particularly interested in mechanization.)

The new Berber recruits trained with a will. Like the veteran Goumiers of the pacification days, their natural forte was scouting and patrolling and the slashing attack. They could move swiftly and silently through the most difficult terrain, and this deadly game was fun for them, particularly when it came to such gory duties as quietly dispatching sentries with their knives.

While it might have been expected that these primitive people would be handy with such simple tools of warfare as rifles, bayonets and knives, there was at first some doubt about their ability to handle the more complex aspects of modern combat. The Goumiers paucity of formal education, however, didn't seem to handicap them very much when it came to learning the use of the more complicated support weapons and communications equipment of World War II. What they lacked in knowledge they made up for in aptitude.

There was never any doubt why the French officers who were training the Goums were so eager to fight. They desperately wanted to redeem the honor of their army after the defeat of 1940 and free their homeland from the occupation of the hated Nazis. Unlike their American and British allies, they actually looked forward to combat; to them killing Germans was a personal thing and everyone they killed was a step nearer home.

The Berbers, on the other hand, had no particular axe to grind. They had nothing against the Germans. They simply liked to fight, and being paid for it was an added attraction. They were mercenaries pure and simple, whose loyalties were not to France but to their officers, for whom they developed a great affection. As they later demonstrated, they would willingly follow them anywhere.

The mountain Berbers, like other devout Muslims, seemed unafraid of death, for they believed that dying in battle gained them immediate entrance into Paradise. To make it easier for Allah to haul them there, they left an extra tuft of hair on top of their heads and many Goumiers had developed this into a little pigtail that peeked below the turban. All were bearded, and this added to their somewhat terrifying appearance—although some of the younger men could only manage a very wispy facial adornment.

Another Berber characteristic was a strong sense of clan or tribe. The French command recognized this and organized the Goums accordingly, tribe by tribe. Traditionally the people of different areas wore distinctive *djellabas* and this, too, the French respected, with several different official patterns representing various regions. While discipline was relatively strict, appearance was not deemed of great importance and the Goumiers were never spit-and-polish parade soldiers. But the Moroccan tribesmen were by nature fighting men, and the French took advantage of this quality to mold their irregulars into what turned out to be one of the most effective corps of mountain infantry anywhere.

The Allied landings on the North African shore in November 1942, brought Major-General George S. Patton, Jr. to Morocco. After a series of short, sharp clashes with the Americans,[17] the French capitulated, and as commander of the Western Task Force, Patton could have become the virtual military dictator of Morocco. He would have gloried in the role, but his iron hand remained in a decidedly velvet glove. While troops of the other task forces that had landed in Oran and Algiers moved on to meet the Germans in Tunisia, Patton's command remained in Morocco to protect the Allied rear against a possible German attack through Spain and Spanish Morocco. Strangely enough, Patton the rough, tough soldier now became the perfect diplomat. He was a Francophile, spoke some French and had in peacetime been a student at the famous French cavalry school in Saumur. During the next few months he became great friends not only with the French resident-general, but with the Arab sultan of Morocco and the Berber pasha of Marrakesh, the latter a local chieftain who controlled the mountain regions of the south. He toured the country, reviewing French native troops whom he admired as much for their colorful uniforms as for their discipline, esprit and soldierly bearing, and he was respected by them in turn.

Inevitably, he was introduced to Colonel Augustin-Léon Guillaume. The meeting was electric. These two aggressive longtime career officers saw eye-to-eye on almost everything. The American with the ivory-handled pistols and the Frenchman in the *djellaba* were indeed cut from the same cloth—and this had a later effect on the combat assignment of the Goums.

"That man," Patton told his interpreter after the meeting, "is worth three divisions!"[18]

During their secret training the Goums had learned to operate in closer concert with each other. Now they were organized as "tabors," battalion-size units of three Goums each. (Henceforth the irregulars were called "the Tabors" almost as often as they were called "the Goums.") These in turn were reassembled, as they had been at the beginning of the war, into *Groupes de Supplétifs Marocains* of three Tabors each. The 1st GSM was mustered at Khenifra in February 1941, the 2nd at Azilal in June, the 3rd at Sefrou in January 1942, and the 4th at Rabat in April. During this period seven other independent Tabors were organized and readied for combat—all this without the knowledge of the Axis commissioners.

At the end of December 1942, not long after the North African French decided to join the Allies, the 1st GSM entrained for Tunisia, as part of the provisional Moroccan Division. A few weeks later the 2nd GSM joined them in the line facing, for the first time, the formidable legions of Adolf Hitler. For the next two-and-a-half years the Moroccan Goumiers would be fighting Germans.

CHAPTER 2

A Legend Is Born

The *feldwebel* who was sergeant-of-the-guard found the sentry in a bloody heap. His throat had been cut, and one ear was missing. Worse yet, two of the panzer grenadiers who had been sleeping near the perimeter of the bivouac area were gone, no doubt taken prisoner. No one had seen or heard anything, but the Germans knew what had happened. It was those damned Moroccans again!

That story was typical of the tales that floated around North Africa after the Goums arrived in Tunisia in the winter of 1942–43. Did the Moroccans actually cut off ears to prove they had killed an enemy? (The ancient Trojans were said to have engaged in the same gruesome practice.) The French officers would deny it or simply shrug their shoulders. Who knows what the tribesmen did in the heat of battle when the officers weren't immediately present? Perhaps it was a good idea to spread the rumor, if only to throw some fear into the enemy. Whether these stories were true or not, the Tunisian campaign was the beginning of the Goumiers' reputation for sheer ferocity.[1]

Tunisia was hard on everybody, but it was particularly hard on the French. From the very first landings of the Americans and British on the North African shores on November 8, 1942, the situation was tragically confusing to the French army. Should they fight the Allied invaders or join them and fight the Germans? The French army in Africa had pledged its oath to Marshal Henri Philippe Pétain, the aged World War I hero who was now the head of the French government in Vichy. He emphatically ordered it to resist the Allies, and most of the French forces, however reluctantly, did so.

Fortuitously, Admiral Jean-François Darlan, second in command to Pétain, was in Algiers visiting his seriously ill son at the time of the invasion, and was taken into custody by the Allies. General Dwight D. Eisenhower, commanding the invasion forces from his headquarters on Gibraltar, sent his deputy, Major-General Mark W. Clark, to convince Darlan to countermand Pétain's orders. It took some doing, but after considerable table-pounding and threats by Clark, Darlan gave in. He ordered a cease-fire, and the fighting across French North Africa came to a halt.

All this was particularly difficult for General George Barré who commanded the French forces in and around Tunis, the chief city of Tunisia. When the Germans heard the news of the Allied invasion they acted with their usual speed and efficiency. Almost immediately German and Italian troops started to pour into Tunis and Bizerte by air and sea.

For a week thereafter the military and political situation was completely confused. German aircraft began to land at once at El Alouina airfield in Tunis and shortly after at Sidi Ahmed in Bizerte, all at a rapid rate. It was only a short flight from their bases in Italy and only a day's journey by ship to the huge port at Bizerte.

Like their compatriots in Algeria and Morocco, the authorities in Tunisia were totally confounded. What should they do? Orders from Marshal Pétain in Vichy told them to cooperate with the Germans. Orders from Darlan in Algiers told them not to. Now Pétain issued orders replacing Darlan with Noguès, the French resident-general in Morocco, but on arriving in Algiers Noguès sided with Darlan.

At first General Barré and Admiral Louis Derrien, who commanded the naval forces with their important base at Bizerte, obeyed Vichy. On hearing of the landings in Algeria and

Morocco they decided to oppose the Allied forces if and when they moved on Tunisia. Barré actually placed a guard of several hundred French soldiers to protect the German planes that were now arriving in such profusion at El Aouina, and he openly criticized the attitude of his officers who were outraged at the German actions.

But by November 10, things had changed. That morning Darlan had declared the cease-fire. That same afternoon Allied planes bombed the El Alouina airfield. Barré withdrew his troops at the field and sent them back to their barracks. Again Pétain disavowed Darlan's cease-fire order, and reaffirmed his own previous orders to resist the Allies. Barré and Derrien conferred, and decided to do nothing. They would observe a strict neutrality and wait to see what happened.

However, by this time the German occupation forces in France had moved into the previously unoccupied zone in the south. According to General Juin, currently the commanding general of all French forces in North Africa (and an Allied sympathizer), this nullified the 1940 armistice. He told Barré and Derrien they could do whatever their consciences demanded. After some quick soul-searching, Barré started to move his troops out of the Tunis area and into the mountains to the west. He now felt he had the go-ahead from his commanding officer, and he had decided to join the Allies. Before the Germans knew what was happening, he had his meager forces emplaced some forty-five miles away, *facing* the rapidly increasing Axis forces.

Derrien's story, on the other hand, was sad. At first he, too, was determined to defy the Axis forces, but, gradually, facing the overwhelming strength of the Germans, he weakened. When the enemy put the pressure on, threatening to slaughter anyone who defied them, he turned the naval base and the port facilities over to the Germans, and was given his freedom to return to France if he wished.[2]

Barré dug in along a generally north-south axis according to plans laid down in 1940 to prevent an invasion of Algeria from the Italians in Libya. The main part of this line extended from Beja through Teboursouk to Le Kef and included some of the more easily defended mountainous regions in the country.

In December the Barré group was reinforced by the arrival of the French XIX Corps under General Louis-Marie Koeltz, which included the provisional Morocco Division (Division de Marche du Maroc) and the leading elements of Goumiers. To accomplish this manpower miracle, the French command, perennially short of troops, scared up 70,000 more soldiers than the Germans thought they had; some creative record keeping had been employed to deceive the German-Italian armistice commission back in 1941. In addition, the previously concealed weapons came out of their hiding places—55,000 rifles, 4,000 automatic weapons, 210 mortars, 43 antitank guns and 82 75mm cannons were added to the French arsenal.[3]

Welcome as these weapons were, there was a downside, for *all* the French armament was obsolete. Their antitank guns were useless against the panzers, their trucks were badly in need of maintenance and were without spare parts, most of the artillery was of World War I vintage, and there was a drastic gasoline shortage besides.

The defense of Tunisia depended largely on the occupation of two mountain ranges, the Eastern Dorsale, ranging due south and petering out in the salt marshes and desert territory of southern Tunisia, and the Western Dorsale, extending in a southwesterly direction across the Algerian border. In the north the mountains intersect and join to form a sort of inverted "V" not far southwest of Tunis.[4]

General Koeltz's XIX Corps took up positions in the Eastern Dorsale, and the terrain into which General Maurice Mathenet's Morocco Division moved was mountainous and wild—Goum country.

Chanting their native songs, this typically cheerful detachment of Moroccan goumiers is led through the Tunisian hills by a young Frenchman. It was in this rugged country that the goumiers first showed their flair for mountain fighting in World War II.

The Germans in the meanwhile were landing tanks, guns and personnel at a furious rate and forming a powerful bridgehead around Tunis and Bizerte, first under command of General Walter Nehring and then under General Hans-Jurgen von Arnim. At the same time the famous "Desert Fox," General Irwin Rommel, was approaching Tunisia from the southeast, pursued all the way from Egypt by the equally well-known General Bernard Montgomery's British Eighth Army. The aim of von Arnim was to land enough men and materiel to defend the bridgehead and stretch the German forces down the east coast of Tunisia to meet and join Rommel's people. The combined forces would then be powerful enough, it was hoped, to push the Allies out of North Africa. It was probably an impossible dream and Rommel knew it. Hitler didn't, however, and the ambitious von Arnim replaced Rommel as the Nazi dictator's favorite general.

The Allied aim was to move enough troops into Tunisia from their landing places in Algeria and Morocco to take back Tunis and Bizerte from the Germans and drive a wedge between von Arnim and Rommel, while Montgomery closed in from the south. But they were nowhere near strong enough yet, and the French were left as a screening force to hold their weak sector of the line with little hope of reinforcement.

It was into this somewhat wobbly line that the Goumiers were thrust—and they proved their worth almost immediately. Where the breakdown of their obsolete materiel seriously hampered the regular French forces, it meant little to the hillmen from Morocco. They were infiltrated along the line as needed, and usually found themselves in the most difficult terrain of the mountainous regions. The failure of French mechanical transport was unimportant to them, they never had any to begin with. In the trackless mountains, their mules and horses were far more valuable than any wheeled vehicle.

The British and Americans also pushed forces into Tunisia. Soon there were scattered tank battles, artillery duels and infantry skirmishes along this north-south line from the forested mountains along the northern coast to the rocky deserts of the south.

Soon after coming into position on the right of Barré's group, Mathenet's Morocco Division was ordered to attack through the mountains toward Tunis, with the eventual objective being the important road junction of Pont du Fahs. Troops selected for this operation were the 3rd Tabor of Lieutenant-Colonel Leblanc's 1st GTM, with another Tabor in reserve, as well as four battalions of Tirailleurs, plus a few pitifully inadequate tanks and some out-of-date artillery.

The attempt was a failure. The Tirailleurs were surprised by the sudden appearance of a large number of enemy tanks and were badly shot up. They were forced to retreat, leaving the Goumiers on their right flank isolated. Repeated Luftwaffe attacks finished the job; the Goumiers had no antiaircraft protection, their liaison with the Allied air forces was poor and German planes ruled the sky. They were ordered to retire.

In analyzing the defeat, French officers believed the leading cause was the unexpected appearance of the German heavy tanks in the mountains where no one had thought they could operate. Then, of course, the few tanks the French had were totally inadequate to meet the threat, antiquated D-1s and Soumas that simply couldn't stand up to the modern Mark IVs and Tigers of the Germans. As for the few French antitank weapons, they were mere pop-guns whose shells just bounced off the German armor.

And yet the French stuck stubbornly to their positions on the Eastern Dorsale. Now they were ordered to hunker down and hold where they were, avoiding pitched battles and waging guerrilla warfare wherever possible. This, of course, suited the Goumiers perfectly. The tribesmen were right in their element as scouts and raiders, silently knifing enemy sentries, snatching prisoners, destroying supply dumps, gathering important intelligence—and then simply disappearing back to their own lines. Among friend and foe alike their reputation for this type of work grew steadily.

Von Arnim, still trying to close the gap on the east coast between his 5th Panzer Army and Rommel's forces, could not allow the continued occupation of the Eastern Dorsale, for the mountains dominated the coastal plain. On January 18 he launched a major attack, which fell heavily on the Moroccan Division. The French fought gallantly, but further weakened by their losses in the previous fighting, they had little chance against the well-equipped and determined Germans.

Taking heavy losses, the Goumiers did their part, but not always successfully. By this time the 2nd GTM had arrived from Morocco and entered the line under command of Lieutenant-Colonel Boyer de Latour, another veteran of the pacification era in Morocco. His offensive-minded attitude was one of the bright spots in an otherwise dark picture. The attack of one of his Goums, the 60th, on a strongly held hill feature called 781, was one of many desperate acts typical of that period at the beginning of 1943 when the French were just hanging by their fingernails to the Eastern Dorsale. It was a carefully planned assault, the very boldness of which augured well for its success. But it all depended on surprise—and an overeager French artillery battery supporting the action fired too soon, alerting the defenders. The result was one more failure, with the Goumiers again taking heavy casualties.

More successful was another typical Goumier action when a Tabor of the 1st GTM ambushed a convoy of twelve German trucks in the vicinity of Djebel Mansour, capturing them all. A welcome bonus in this attack was the fact that the trucks were loaded with French POWs who were freed to fight again.

But that was just a minor victory in a sea of disappointment. The French were weakening and their sector of the front was at the point of complete collapse. The high command, Giraud and his staff, was endeavoring to raise and train new French levies, and no matter how much they were needed, there were simply no reserves to be had. Giraud called on the Americans for help. General Lloyd R. Fredenhall, II Corps commander, responded with Combat Command "B" of the 1st Armored Division, a powerful unit of about 3,500 men with tanks, tank destroyers and artillery. CCB was commanded by Brigadier-General Paul M. Robinett, an ideal choice for the job since he not only had the experience of fighting the Germans in northern Tunisia, but he spoke French and before the war had attended the French *École de Guerre* in Paris and the Cavalry School at Saumur. He understood French military philosophy, and their methods and tactics were familiar to him. The arrival of CCB stabilized the French sector of the front and helped prevent the immediate collapse of the French forces.

But by the end of January more heavy enemy attacks put severe pressure on the battered French, and the evacuation of the Eastern Dorsale began. The Goums retreated across the plain with the rest of the army and into the hills and valleys of the Western Dorsale, where they took up new positions. Sometimes in the confusion of the withdrawal communications failed and units became lost—on both sides of the line. In mid-February a Moroccan Tabor was reported among the Allied troops playing hide-and-seek with a lost unit of the 10th Panzer Division that had wandered into the Bou Chebka area when the Americans were having their hard time at Kasserine Pass a few miles to the north.[5]

Kasserine was the high water mark for the Axis forces in Tunisia. Stopped by British armor and American artillery, short of replacements (and everything else), they had simply run out of steam. After that, General Rommel, who had left his command near the Libyan border to plan and lend his hand in the Kasserine assault, turned about and returned to southern Tunisia to face Montgomery once again. Shortly thereafter he went back to Germany on sick leave, never to return to

Africa. Von Arnim remained in overall Axis command in the north of Tunisia, with the Italian General Messe in charge of the Italo-German forces facing Montgomery in the south.

After that, heavy rains, mud and generally miserable weather closed down the Tunisian campaign for the rest of the winter. When the fighting started up again in the spring, the Allies had been reinforced and completely reorganized. The tactical mess that had handicapped the Allied forces, with Americans, British and French all tangled together, had been straightened out. Supply difficulties had been overcome and troop reinforcements and new equipment had greatly added to Allied strength. The German and Italian forces that had been pursued by General Montgomery's Eighth Army all the way from Egypt into southern Tunisia had succeeded in joining with von Arnim's army and both were now battling desperately to hold a line based on Enfidaville on the coast and forming a wide circle around Tunis and Bizerte.

In the wake of the American debacle at Kasserine, Fredendall had been relieved. He had been replaced by Patton who, after reinvigorating II Corps and directing it at El Guettar, Gafsa and Maknassy, went back to Morocco to finish planning for the invasion of Sicily. Major-General Omar Bradley was named II Corps commander for the final Tunisian battles, but you can see the fine Italian hand of Patton somewhere in the background when the 4th Moroccan Tabor, an independent unit of Goumiers, was attached to the Americans for the rest of the campaign.

The new arrangements had the American II Corps transferred from the south to the extreme north of the line with the object of taking Bizerte, while the British, in the center, were aimed at Tunis. General Koeltz's French XIX Corps, with its two *Groupes* of Goumiers, had the job of clearing out the mountainous region southwest of that city. Montgomery's Eighth Army was moving swiftly toward Sfax, but was unprepared to leave the coast and fight in the mountains.[6]

Koeltz opened his part of the spring campaign with an attack on the Axis forces now holding the Eastern Dorsale near the passes of Pichon and Fondouk. De Latour's 2nd Group of Goumiers was ordered to drive the enemy troops off the Djebel Ouselltia while Leblanc's 1st GTM attacked in the hill masses further north. The goal was to sweep the enemy troops out of the mountains, clearing the gaps that opened onto the holy city of Kairouan and the coastal plain.

The assault, which began in early April, was eminently successful. The fighting covered the very same mountains where the French had been so severely punished in January, and the Goumiers were eager for revenge. Although they hadn't been reequipped to the same extent as their Allies, at least this time they had enough ammunition. It was payback time, a matter the Goumiers took seriously; their blood was up and they were fighting mad.

Charging up the mountainside, the 7th Tabor, an independent unit attached to the 2nd GTM, was the first of the Moroccans to fall upon the German defenders, killing forty-two and taking sixty prisoners. At almost the same time the 1st Tabor took the strongpoint of Le Kef es Snouber and after much hard fighting hurtled down the east side of the *djebel* to attack the rear and flank of the enemy troops defending l'Argoub el Negrila. The Germans and Italians continued their desperate resistance, but by 1000 hours in the morning of the twelfth, that sector of the Eastern Dorsale was back in French hands. The *embordement rapide* of de Latour's Goumiers had completely unbalanced the enemy.

In the meanwhile, the northward push of Leblanc and his 1st GTM had meant equally swift destruction for the Axis forces in their path. In Wild West fashion a mounted platoon of the group's 2nd Tabor captured 110 of the enemy east of Ben Hadjar, the 12th Tabor rounded up another 118, while the 3rd Tabor picked up 205 more enlisted men and 6 officers of the crack Italian Superga Division, which was rapidly disintegrating.

The swift advance of the Goumiers soon turned the methodical retreat of the Axis forces into a disorganized rout. The 1st GTM ended its sortie through the mountains a few miles east of Karamchoum, with the enemy pushed off the Dorsale and back into the coastal plain. Revenge was, indeed, sweet.[7]

Farther north, the independent 4th Tabor, having been attached to the American II Corps found itself assigned, along with some other assorted French units, to the U.S. 9th Division for the assault on Bizerte with its huge naval base. The French contingent was under command of the dapper Colonel Goislard de Monsabert, whose snow white hair and moustache, short stature and generous proportions gave him the aspect of a beardless Santa Claus—but his reputation as a fierce and fearless commander belied his benign appearance.[8]

Taking part in the recapture of Bizerte was an important assignment for the Goums, for the naval base in that northeastern corner of Tunisia had been the pride of the French Mediterranean fleet. The surrender of its coastal defenses, shipyards and port facilities to the Germans without a fight that past November was a disgrace that weighed on the French military almost as heavily as the defeat of 1940. Giraud was perfectly willing to put this small group of French troops under direct American control just to play a part in regaining this significant French asset.

The Goumiers lived up to their reputation. They fought through the hills on the approach to Bizerte in their usual bold and aggressive manner and with their seeming contempt for death. They fought along the north side of Lake Achtel alongside the Americans, and they battled down the palm lined boulevards of the city amid the devastation of the bombed-out buildings. For awhile the defenders, too, fought with the desperation of doomed men. They had sown a witches seed of mines and booby traps in advance of their attackers, and at the very end some of them resisted hand-to-hand. And then the resistance suddenly collapsed completely. When it was all over and the last German alive had surrendered, it was the Goumiers who triumphantly raised the tricolor over the main fortress of Bizerte.[9]

That was on the afternoon of May 7. On the same day the British entered Tunis, and it seemed the war in North Africa was finally over.

But not quite. Stubborn German units, including remnants of the Afrika Korps and the 21st Panzer Division, were still holding out in the tangled wilds of the forbidding Zaghouan *massif* just south of Tunis. In an epic final battle, the Goumiers of Koeltz's XIX Corps, right at home in those rugged heights, flushed out their old antagonists with bayonet, grenade and knife. On May 12, not far from the ruins of the ancient Roman aqueduct at Zaghouan, the last of the Germans in that area surrendered to General Mathenet. The Tunisian campaign was now definitely over.

In the last weeks of the fighting, the Goumiers had shown themselves to be more than mere raiders and behind-the-lines cutthroats. In open warfare they performed as first-class infantry, every bit equal in skill, determination and élan to the best the Germans had to offer. And in the more difficult mountains where the enemy couldn't take advantage of his superiority in tanks and artillery, they were better.

On May 13, 1943, General Harold Alexander, commander of all Allied forces in Tunisia, sent a brief message to his prime minister, Winston Churchill. With typical British aplomb he announced: "Sir, it is my duty to report that the Tunisian Campaign is over. All enemy resistance has ceased. We are masters of the North African shores."

The Tunisian Campaign made the Goumiers well known to all the Allied commanders, and the Moroccans had reason to march proudly as they passed the reviewing stand in the victory parade in Tunis. They were well pleased with their reception. British, Americans, Australians, New Zealanders, Indians, Gurkhas and others had taken part in the great battles from El

Alamein to Tunis and Bizerte, but according to historian George F. Howe, "French troops were prominent among the marchers with the warmest applause going to the Moroccan *goumiers*."[10]

One important reason for the Goumiers' success in battle was that the French high command already knew of their fighting qualities and gave them the opportunity to demonstrate those unusual abilities right from the start. After all, the commander of the French armed forces was General Henri Giraud, the tall sixty-four-year-old fighter with the startling blue eyes and the bristling moustache. Giraud, who had been a prisoner of war in two world wars and an escapee in both, had served most of his military life between those wars in North Africa. He had been commander of one of the *Groupes Mobiles* in the final phase of the Moroccan pacification; he knew the Berbers and he knew the Goums. As a result he always tried to promote their use, particularly in mountainous areas, and he heartily recommended them to the other Allied commanders. He visited their camps and reviewed their units whenever he could. Throughout the French army he was known as "*Giraud l'Africaine*."[11]

General Alphonse Juin, the officer who, under Giraud, commanded all the French ground forces in North Africa, was another veteran of the colonial wars. He, too, was an enthusiastic promoter of the Goums and used them whenever possible. Later in the war he was named commander of the powerful FEC (French Expeditionary Corps) that played such a spectacular part in the drive on Rome, and he made sure the Goumiers were an important part of the operation.

Other Allied generals, too, became aware of the military possibilities of the Moroccans. In his memoirs General Omar Bradley acknowledged the aid of the "fierce Berber tribesmen" who joined his forces in capturing Bizerte,[12] and British general Brian Horrocks, one of Montgomery's ablest corps commanders, also remarked on their toughness under difficult conditions. When Horrocks was severely wounded in an air raid and lying in the hospital in Bizerte, he observed the reactions of other patients to their sufferings. He later remarked: "I occupied the corner of a general ward with a constantly changing population of troops from every country, friend and foe. The toughest of all, unquestionably, were the French goumier from the North African mountains, on whom pain and discomfort seem to have no effect whatever."[13]

But for the Goumiers, the most important general at the moment was George Patton, now in Morocco planning for his Seventh Army's part in the invasion of Sicily. He had seen the Goumiers in action in Tunisia, and he remembered his meeting with the dynamic Colonel Guillaume. A Francophile since his experiences in World War I, he wanted French troops under his command, but most of these were in the early stages of training with new and unfamiliar American equipment and were not yet ready for combat. Nevertheless, Patton asked for at least one token battalion of French troops, specifically the *4th Tabor Marocain,* which had fought alongside the Americans at Bizerte. Giraud, always anxious to have his people demonstrate their martial skills, agreed, Eisenhower approved and the 4th Tabor, just back in Morocco after its successes in Tunisia, was ordered to join Patton's forces.

At Sefrou, its home garrison, the Tabor was hastily issued its new American equipment, with which the Goumiers were delighted. The olive-drab uniforms, G.I. shoes and canvas leggings replaced worn and tattered undergarments and goatskin sandals, but the Moroccans overall appearance was essentially unchanged. They continued to wear the traditional *djellaba,* as did all the Goumiers throughout the war.

On July 5 the 4th Tabor, commanded by Captain Verlet,[14] left from Bizerte and on the fourteenth disembarked at Licata, Sicily. Its strength was 58 French officers and non-coms and 678 Berbers, plus 117 horses and 126 mules.

The Sicilian Campaign, code-named "Husky," was a confused affair from the start. In the first place there was considerable discussion about whether or not the island should be invaded at all—perhaps the first goal in penetrating Hitler's "Festung Europa" should be Sardinia or Corsica. Both of these islands flanked Italy rather than lying at its toe, and an invasion from either would avoid a long and costly struggle up the Italian boot. Or should the Allies forget the Mediterranean altogether and concentrate all their power on an attack on the west coast of France, which was the American preference? However, now that the Axis troops had been chased out of North Africa, that continent had remained a perfect base for Churchill's choice of an assault on the "soft underbelly" of Europe, and the Americans finally went along with the idea.

The initial plan called for simultaneous landings over widely scattered parts of the island, and that strategy was generally agreed upon by all, British and Americans alike—until General Montgomery, who was to command one of the Allied armies involved, vigorously objected. He predicted disaster unless the attack was concentrated on the southeast section of the island, and such was his prestige at the time that his suggestion was adopted by General Alexander, the overall commander, even though the other planners disagreed. In the event, on July 10 the Allied troops landed in a concentrated line with the British stretched from Syracuse to Cape Pachino and the Americans continuing along the southern coast to Licata.[15]

The landings were at first successful, with the Italian coast defense troops making little effort to stop the Allied penetration. Most of these were Sicilian natives who surrendered in droves or simply changed into civilian clothes and disappeared into the populace. Then for awhile it was touch-and-go for the American 1st Division near Gela when it was attacked over the beaches by tanks of the Hermann Goering Panzer Division, but the enemy armor was eventually driven off by naval gunfire. By the time the Goumiers arrived, Licata, after some bloody fighting by the 3rd Division, had been secured.

The subsequent planning of the Sicilian Campaign was very sketchy indeed—in fact, there seemed to be no detailed plan at all. The overall commander was the British General Sir Harold Alexander and under him was Montgomery's famous Eighth Army and the untried American Seventh Army, commanded by the mercurial General Patton. The general idea was for Montgomery to push up the east side of the island to Messina to cut off the German and Italian garrisons and prevent them from escaping to the Italian mainland, while Patton's troops moved up the center, acting as a flank guard for the British.

Patton did not like this subsidiary role at all. He requested Alexander's permission to probe northwest toward Palermo, and then turned this reconnaissance-in-force into a full-fledged attack on that city. To do this he formed a "provisional corps" composed of the 3rd Infantry Division, the 2nd Armored Division and the 82nd Airborne Division, all under his deputy, Major-General Geoffrey Keyes, and started them off toward Palermo some hundred mountainous miles away. The 4th Tabor joined this group at Agrigento with the mission of securing the eastern flank of the Agrigento-Palermo main Highway (Route 118). Attached to the 15th Infantry Regiment of Major-General Lucian Truscott's hard marching 3rd Division, the Goumiers were right at home as they pushed on into the rugged Sicilian hill country.

According to Hanson W. Baldwin, military correspondent of the New York Times, Sicily was "no soft and flabby gateway [to Europe]. The stormily beautiful and harshly patterned island was, in July 1943, as it had been for thousands of years, a rugged, ridged, sun-baked land as inhospitable in terrain and climate and primitive communications to the Allied invaders as it had been to Greeks, Carthaginians and Romans." The Goumiers found it hellishly hot, unbelievably dusty—and malarial besides.

Truscott had trained his men to the very pinnacle of physical fitness. The 3rd Division troops were famous throughout the army for being able to march for long distances at five miles per hour instead of the usual three—the so-called Truscott Trot. But for the Moroccans marching through the mountains on Truscott's flank, maintaining that pace was no problem at all.

After a punishing march and some skirmishes with retreating Italians, the Tabor reached Mount Vito on July 19 and continued on into the night to Cammerata and beyond. At dawn they were slowed down by determined Bersaglieri dug in on the heights above the Plantane Valley. When this force was dealt with, the Tabor was ordered to march as rapidly as possible to the hills south of Lercada Fridi, there to extend across the main road to keep it closed to the enemy. They accomplished this mission after another trying night march, and elements of the American infantry occupied the town itself the next day.

But the 4th Tabor was kept moving and reached Corleone on the twenty-second just as Palermo fell.[16] At last the Goumiers were rewarded with a short rest, after nearly one hundred miles of forced marching through difficult mountain terrain.

Men and animals were exhausted, but their well-earned repose did not last long. In central Sicily the American 1st Division was meeting strong opposition, and on the twenty-fifth the Goums were off to help. They were immediately attached to the 18th Infantry operating in the mountains above Nicosia and their job was to protect the regiment's left flank. On the morning of the twenty-seventh the Tabor reached Gangi and then moved on to the 5,700-foot Mount Sambighi. It was a tough nut to crack against stiffening resistance, but by the end of the following day the Goumiers had cleaned out the enemy's mountain strongholds.

The 66th Goum was now ordered to attack enemy positions on Mount Caniglia, occupied by Italian infantry of the Aosta Division. This was to be no easy mission. Not only was the terrain as difficult as any the Goumiers had yet encountered in Sicily, but a heavy fog and lack of time had prevented the thorough reconnaissance that had become a hallmark of Goumier tactics. Nevertheless, with their usual élan the Goumiers hurled themselves at the well-entrenched Aosta. This time the enemy did not just melt away, and in fact there were a great deal more of them than the Moroccans had reckoned with. Pretty soon the 66th Goum was in big trouble. The fighting became desperate, and the Goumiers called for help. The rest of the Tabor responded quickly and succeeded in getting the surrounded Goum out of its difficulty, but only after taking heavy casualties. By the end of the next morning, however, the Goumiers had their revenge as the Italians were flushed off the mountainside, and the Mistretta-Sperlinga Road was reached, enabling the division to take Nicosia.

But there was no rest for the weary. On July 30 the Goumiers continued eastward toward Capizzi in the mountains north of Route 120. Route 120 is a vital artery running toward Messina. It is about twenty miles inland from the northern coast of the island, and the enemy rear guards were fighting hard along this important axis of their retreat. They succeeded in holding up the 68th Goum with heavy machine-gun and mortar fire—but not for long. The rest of the Tabor, plus the 2nd Battalion of the 18th Infantry, came up to support the 68th, and the enemy resistance was overcome by nightfall. On the morning of the thirty-first, Capizzi was occupied and 241 Italian soldiers were captured. Strangely, among the prisoners were two Alsatians who asked to fight in the ranks of the Moroccans! How they came to be with the Italians is not recorded, but in the general confusion of the retreat it can be surmised that German and Italian troops had become intermingled, and it was then that the Alsatians found their opportunity.

The Tabor continued to secure the flank of the American infantry moving toward Mount Acuto—and that's when things started coming apart. The Italian regiments had just about disintegrated, and now the Goumiers had run into the strongest of the German defensive positions, around Troino. The 67th Goum leading the advance was held up by heavy German machine-gun fire, while the 68th Goum, also under fire, managed to establish a tenuous defensive position on the mountainside. As night fell the order was given to break off contact. German artillery fire was intense and accurate, and in this action the Tabor suffered major punishment.

The next day was worse. Contact with the division was lost for seven hours, and the Tabor endured the friendly fire of American artillery firing counter battery, whose gunners didn't know where the Goumiers were. Liaison with the Royal Air Force was also terrible that day (as it was throughout the entire Sicilian campaign) and a group of Spitfires machine-gunned the Tabor unmercifully.[17]

Somehow the Goumiers survived. The 1st Division was relieved by the 9th Division,[18] the 4th Tabor's old comrades from the Tunisian campaign, and the Goumiers continued stolidly on their flank-guard advance. It was, as usual, "one damn mountain after another" as the Moroccans progressed by successive bounds from peak to peak and ridge to ridge through the Sicilian highlands, eventually coming to the Randazzo-Nazo-Cap Orlando Road. At that point they were ordered to halt. The Allies had captured Messina, and as far as the Goums were concerned, the Sicilian campaign was over.

The conquest of Sicily was hailed at the time as a great Allied victory, but the battalion-size contribution of French

Moroccan troops is scarcely mentioned in the popular history books.[19] Actually, while the island became useful for its airfields and ports and as a springboard for future Mediterranean operations, the escape of the Axis forces with most of their equipment put something of a damper on the victory. The Goumiers, however, had fought well and added to their reputation among their peers as superb mountain infantry.

Their exploits in Sicily were rewarded on August 19 by a visit from General Giraud. *Giraud l'Africaine*, true to form, revued the 4th Tabor at their bivouac area at Guardiola, bringing with him the congratulations and salute of France and her allies. The latter were represented by General Bradley himself and by General Manton S. Eddy, commander of the 9th Division. The Tabor left Sicily from Palermo (which it had helped to capture but had never previously seen) on September 4 and returned to Morocco. There was a victory parade down the streets of Fez before an enthusiastic crowd, but just being home was reward enough for the Goumiers.

What had the men of the 4th Tabor accomplished for themselves in Sicily? For one thing, they had "shown the *djellaba*," as well as the tricolor, to both enemy and ally. Then, in winning more laurels for the Moroccan Goums in general, they had also gained experience in fighting Germans, know-how that would come in handy to the troops in training at home. They had learned more about dealing with the terrifying artillery, automatic weapons, tanks, mines and booby traps their now and future enemy was so expert in using—and they had the satisfaction of teaching their foe a few new tricks of their own. It was their first adventure overseas, the first time in their history they had fought outside Africa. It was also an opportunity to learn new techniques, like transporting large numbers of horses and mules by ship, always a tricky business and a skill they would soon use again. And in a larger sense, they had overcome what may have been something of an inferiority complex, a sense of being "country bumpkins" fit to fight only in African wars. One way or another, for the Moroccan irregulars Sicily was an important breakthrough.

The fall of Sicily left two major islands in the central Mediterranean still occupied by Axis forces—Sardinia and Corsica. Sicily, however, had proven the death knell of Italy's alliance with the Third Reich, and the two forces were now, in September 1943, facing each other as enemies. On both islands fighting had broken out.

On Sardinia the Germans were in grave difficulties. They had only one division on the island, against two Italian infantry divisions, three coast defense divisions and a parachute division. But the 90th Panzer Grenadier Division had all the attributes of a former Afrika Korps unit and its commander, Lieutenant-General Lungerhausen, was a typically efficient German officer. When the order came for the Germans to evacuate the island, all the ill-equipped and scattered Italian troops could do was harass the Germans on their march to the evacuation ports and watch them sail across the Straits of Bonifacio, virtually unscathed, to Corsica.

Corsica was another matter. At first the German high command was determined to hold it, and Lieutenant-General Albert Kesselring, commander in southern Italy, had sent Major-General von Senger und Etterlin to organize its defense. Besides the 90th Panzer Grenadier Division from Sardinia, he also had the SS Reichsfuehrer Brigade under his command, as well as some Luftwaffe fighter units. But Corsica was a part of France, and its inflamed inhabitants had organized a resistance with some 10,000 automatic weapons air dropped into the wild Corsican countryside at night and secretly distributed to resistance groups in the major cities. When these forces rose up and the Germans felt their sting, it was decided to evacuate the island. Von Senger consolidated his forces and headed for the most likely evacuation port, Bastia, in the northeast corner nearest to Italy.

The Corsicans appealed for help in stopping them. General Giraud replied by assembling a tiny scratch force of French troops and a miniscule fleet of French warships to transport this ad hoc army the 500 miles across the Mediterranean from North Africa to Corsica. He had appealed to his Allies for more substantial help, but it was a bad time; all the available American and British troops were tied up in the invasion of the Italian mainland, as was all the shipping.

So it was that the battered and worn French cruisers *Montcalm* and *Jeanne d'Arc*, the destroyers *Fantasque* and *Terrible* and the torpedo boats *Têmpete* and *Alcyon* were turned into temporary transports. They braved the attacks of the Luftwaffe to ferry the French troops to Ajaccio on the west coast of Corsica. These warriors would seem to be barely adequate in numbers and equipment for the job in hand, consisting mainly of a regiment of Tirailleurs, two squadrons of Spahis (with antiquated tanks and armored cars), some mountain artillery—and the *2nd Groupe de Tabors Marocains*, the latter still under command of the redoubtable Colonel Boyer de Latour.

The 2nd Group was now a different outfit than when its people had gone off to war against the Italians on the Libyan border in 1940. Since then it had endured the disgrace of the 1940 armistice and the subsequent contempt of the Italo-German armistice commission. It had been transformed from a native police force into a trained, disciplined infantry unit. It had suffered severe losses in the early Tunisian campaigns in the Dorsales, but had recovered its pride and found itself again when it beat the best the Germans had to offer in the final weeks of the North African fighting. Now it was a tough, confident, thoroughly professional fighting force, eager to get at the Germans once more. As a sign of this increasing morale there was a new addition to each Goumier's uniform. It was a metal unit insignia depicting the profile of a grinning Goumier with the motto, in French, "Who Laughs Last Laughs Best"—a grim reminder to the enemy of past Moroccan successes.[20]

Corsica is all mountains, covered with that distinctive scrubby brush known as "maquis."[21] General Henry Martin, the leader of the little French expedition of less than 10,000, sent his motorized forces up the few roads in pursuit of the now retreating Germans, while the Goumiers went over the mountains to hit them on the flanks. The fighting developed into a race for Bastia, and the Germans reached there first. Struggling over the mountains, the Goumiers, as usual, had the toughest terrain to traverse and suffered the heaviest losses, particularly as they approached Bastia from the west. To safeguard his troops boarding the evacuation ships, von Senger had spread strong forces in the mountains surrounding the city, and the Goumiers had to rout them out in heavy fighting. In this phase the Tabors had 40 dead, including 3 officers and 124 wounded, 6 officers among them.[22]

But the Germans suffered heavily, too. In addition to their losses in the ground fighting, many of their evacuation ships were hit by French planes and naval vessels. While the Germans managed to evacuate a large portion of their personnel and some of their equipment, the Allies remained in possession of the island with its potentially valuable airfields. In a few months there were seventeen such fields, a useful base in future operations against Italy and southern France.

The fighting ended in October, but the 2nd Group of Tabors was to remain on security duty in Corsica for many months. They hated it; they wanted to fight Germans, and they were particularly chagrined when in January they heard that three other groups of Tabors were leaving North Africa for Italy where the main action was now taking place.

They needn't have worried. As the war progressed, there would be plenty of fighting left for them to do.

CHAPTER 3

Italy—Triumph and Disgrace

From its very beginnings, the American Fifth Army was destined to have a great affect on the French forces in North Africa. Activated under command of Lieutenant-General Mark W. Clark on January 5, 1943, at Oudjda, Morocco, its first mission was to cooperate with French military and civil forces in maintaining order in Morocco and in the western part of Algeria. In addition—and more important for the Goums—it was to "assist in organizing, equipping and training" the French army. In the latter case, emphasis was on the handling of the American equipment that was being supplied to the new French divisions and the Tabors in North Africa.[1] To depict its association with that part of the world, the Fifth Army's new shoulder patch insignia had a distinctly North African motif, with the figures 5A superimposed over a Moorish architectural design.

Although at this time the Goums had just begun fighting in Tunisia, by July they were back in Morocco and training hard under the watchful eye of Colonel Guillaume. While the Goums for the most part were still "irregulars," they were somewhat less so than the "supplétifs," the auxiliaries that had policed the Atlas and gone off to war in Tunisia. Now they had American weapons—rifles, Thompson submachine guns, BARs, light machine guns and mortars—and were considered ready for modern warfare.[2]

While the French were grateful for their new equipment, they resented what they considered to be the restrictions that went along with the transfer. Before the materiel was handed over, the Americans insisted that the French reorganize their divisions along American lines to simplify supply and liaison. Compared with French practice American units had a very large administrative "tail," with a high proportion of supply services in relation to its actual fighting men. To the French this was wasteful, particularly as it affected the African troops who were used to living and fighting under the harshest conditions without the luxury of so many depots, workshops and other ancillary units. Their attitude was, "We don't need all this stuff. Just give us the weapons and let us get on with the fighting." The French brass was particularly annoyed because they had to break up some famous regiments and turn their personnel into service troops to conform to American tables of organization.[3] While all this caused some hard feelings between the French and Americans, the Goumiers really didn't care. They were delighted with their deadly new toys.

Now four groups of Moroccan Tabors were put at the disposition of the Allied command for service in Europe, the 1st, 2nd, 3rd and 4th GTM, with the 2nd soon off to Corsica. To coordinate the activities of these units with the staff of the regular army and the residence general of Morocco, and to facilitate their role in the Allied armies, in July 1943 a new entity was created—the *Commandment des Goums Marocains*. And of course Colonel Augustin-Léon Guillaume was named its commandant.

The entire CGM, most of which was to become part of Clark's Fifth Army, was composed of:

1,077 Frenchmen (246 officers, 727 sergeants and corporals and 104 lance-corporals)

12,570 Moroccans (924 *moquaddem* [sergeants], 1,683 *maoun* [corporals] and 9,963 Goumiers)

Each group had a headquarters and service Goum and each of the three Tabors in the group had a section of four 81 mm mortars. In addition each individual Goum was equipped with two light machine guns and a 60 mm mortar.[4]

It was during this time when the Fifth Army was training in North Africa for the invasion of Italy (code named "Avalanche") that General Clark first met Guillaume and, like Patton, he was impressed. In his memoirs he tells this story:

> General Juin arrived in Mostaganem and prepared to take part in the Italian campaign with the 2nd Moroccan Infantry Division and the 3rd Algerian Infantry Division, in addition to a force of Goumiers, the famous French Moroccan fighters.
>
> The eagerness of the French to fight in the Italian campaign was illustrated by a story that arose when I was looking for some good fighters to undertake a hazardous mission during the AVALANCHE operations. There was a small town north of Salerno where we knew a big ammunition dump was located, and I thought that a band of parachute troops could be dropped there to destroy it. I asked Colonel A.L. Guillaume if he could recommend a group for the mission and he suggested the Goumiers, native soldiers who are extremely clever at knife work.
>
> He offered to investigate and a few days later said that he had fifty volunteers for the job, but that he had a little trouble explaining the job to them about their transportation because none of them had ever been in an airplane.
>
> They wanted to be sure the plane would fly close to the ground and that it would slow down when they jumped," he said.
>
> "Tell them," I replied, "that on such an operation the plane can slow down to about a hundred miles an hour, but it can't fly less than four hundred feet from the ground or their parachutes won't have time to open."
>
> "Yes," said Guillaume, "I told him that. And that's where the confusion began. When I explained about

the parachutes, their leader said, "Praise Allah! Do we get parachutes, too?"[5]

It's a good story—so good in fact that it has been taken up by others, and the very same tale has been told about the Gurkhas of the Indian army. Was it originally a true Goumier story or had Guillaume heard it elsewhere and was simply pulling Clark's leg? At any rate, the Goumiers were never used as paratroopers and the story has become apochryphal.[6]

The Fifth Army landed on the European mainland at Salerno in September 1943 and started fighting its way up the mountainous Italian boot. In October a combined Franco-American commission in North Africa started inspecting the newly reorganized and reequipped Goums and found them ready to join the fighting. The inspectors reported that the French officers and non-coms knew their business very well indeed, the Goumiers were thoroughly familiar with their new American weapons, morale was high and all ranks had an ardent desire to fight as soon as possible.[7] The attitude of the Moroccans toward the Germans had changed somewhat after the Tunisian campaign; it had become more personal, and the Nazi commissioners' previous contempt for the Goumiers had finally sunk in and begun to rankle. This was bad news for the Germans.

In November the 4th GTM was the first of the Tabors to embark for Italy, followed in January 1944 by the 3rd GTM. What they found in their new battleground was not encouraging. Since the hard fought landing at Salerno the American and British troops had been battling their way in a generally northwestern direction toward the "glittering prize" of Rome. The slowly retreating Germans had contested the Allied advance every inch of the way and were masters of defensive warfare. Their greatest ally was the terrain. Throughout Italy great mountain ranges were punctuated by swollen, swift-running

The goumiers join their womenfolk in the abandoned farmhouse where they are quartered on the Italian battlefield. These Moroccan women were brought over from North Africa on U.S. Navy LSTs in a unique modern reenactment of an ancient military tradition—the camp follower.

streams and rivers. These natural barriers were all defended by determined rear guards in carefully positioned strong points protected by interlocking machine gun fire and cleverly hidden mortars and artillery in addition to thousands of mines and miles of barbed wire. Also benefitting the Germans was the horrendous weather; in the fall torrential and continuing rain and biting winds, turning into winter snows and frigid cold, were all infinitely harder on the attackers than on the defenders who were snuggled down in their carefully prepared positions.

When the first elements of General Juin's French Expeditionary Corps (FEC), including two groups of Goumiers, reached their initial battle positions they found that they were up against what was to be called the Germans' Winter Line. This was a system of temporary field fortifications strung across Italy to act as a holding line while the famous Todt labor organization finished constructing the more permanent Gustav line with its linchpin on the crest of Monte Cassino.

The first of the FEC troops to arrive at the front was the 2nd Moroccan Division with the 4th GTM attached. It was positioned in the high mountains at the extreme right of the Fifth Army line. There, after a series of exhausting hill battles, the American troops, neophytes at mountain warfare, had been stopped cold against the newly reinforced Germans. As far as mountain fighting was concerned the Goumiers were at no such disadvantage. The Italian peaks and ridges, which had come as a shock to even those Allied troops who thought they had seen mountains in Tunisia and Sicily, meant nothing to the Moroccans. In their very first engagement they made considerable gains, pushing back the German 5th Mountain Division, which had been hastily thrown into the line against them. In January the 3rd Algerian Division joined the Moroccans, and the Allied line in the FEC sector was advanced an astounding distance[8] through the worst of the mountains north of Cassino, right up to the very back door of the Gustav Line. The

French troops penetrated the German positions and took 1,200 prisoners but had no reserves to follow up this remarkable gain.

Now the Allied high command decided that it was too late to break through the line to the Liri Valley, the "gateway to Rome," before spring. After months of savage fighting under the worst of conditions, the Allied troops were exhausted. They had taken tremendous casualties and there were no more reinforcements. An entire army corps of American and British troops had been taken out of the line to rehearse for the landing at Anzio some miles up the Italian coast. There were very few troops left for offensive action on the Cassino front.

Still, attempts were made. The French continued their activities in the north and kept the Germans worried, while British X Corps made a successful crossing of the Garigliano River and established a valuable bridgehead well to the south. American attempts to cross the Rapido a little way downstream from Monte Cassino were a total failure, ending in disaster for the attackers. Attempts at storming Monte Cassino itself only led to more slaughter, and the rubble left in the wake of the abbey's bombardment by Allied planes only made a better defensive position for the Germans. The landings at Anzio at the end of January were met by German reinforcements called in from northern Italy, France and Hungary. For a while it was touch and go for the Allies on the beachhead—and then stalemate.

The Allied command finally decided that Rome was not going to be taken that winter and settled down to reinforce and reorganize for a spring campaign. The plan was to maintain a thin holding force of British and British-sponsored troops on the Adriatic side of the peninsula directly under control of General Alexander's Fifteenth Army Group, which also controlled both Allied armies in Italy. The British Eighth Army was to move south to take over the Cassino front and be prepared to make the main effort of the spring campaign. It was to break through the Gustav Line and continue through the Liri River valley toward Rome.

The Americans and the French, both part of Clark's Fifth Army, were to take over the southern section of the line with the newly arrived U.S. 88th and 85th Divisions on the extreme left. The FEC was to move from its northern positions into the Garigliano bridgehead, relieving the British X Corps, which was to join the main body of the Eighth Army.

The purpose of these movements was to keep together those troops supplied and administered by the British, such as the Canadians, the Indians, the Poles and the New Zealanders, while the French, organized along American lines, were to stay under Fifth Army command. The only exceptions were the two British Divisions at Anzio, which remained in the Fifth Army.

Now as spring broke through, new units were added to the FEC. The 4th Moroccan Mountain Division had arrived in February and the 1st French Motorized Division landed in Italy in April, as did another group of Tabors, the 1st GTM. While the Mountain Division and the Goumiers held their sections of the line, the 2nd Moroccan and 3rd Algerian Divisions were relieved of their front line duties to carry out further mountain training in the Salerno area. When they returned to the Garigliano sector in May, all was ready for the big spring push. It was code named "Diadem" and was set for May 11.

As that day approached, General Juin stood on the banks of the Garigliano and gazed westward into the mist-shrouded Aurunci Mountains, which his French Expeditionary Corps would have to penetrate on its way to Rome. The Aurunci was a tangled mass of forbidding peaks and treacherous gullies that the high commands of both Allied and German armies considered virtually impenetrable. There were no real roads and very few tracks. The FEC was assigned to that area because it was the only Allied force with troops trained and equipped for mountain warfare, and even then some Allied leaders had grave doubts that Juin's people could keep up with the other troops attacking through less discouraging terrain.

At first it had been planned to go around the highest and most difficult parts of the Aurunci, avoiding the trackless, rock-bound Petrella Massif, but Juin had objected. Intelligence reports had indicated that the territory was only lightly defended. The Germans were relying on the mountains themselves as a sufficient barrier; they thought that no one could get through those impossible heights in any effective force. Juin thought otherwise. He counted on the mountaineering ability of his North Africans, particularly on Guillaume and his Goums, to fight their way through the worst of the hill country. And he relied on the sheer determination of the Frenchmen of his command to defeat the hated Boche. He finally convinced his superiors to let him do it his way.

The Germans had constructed a secondary string of field fortifications about six miles behind the Gustav Line. Called the Adolf Hitler Line, along with its subsidiary Dora extension, it was designed to stop whatever Allied troops could push through the original barriers anchored on Monte Cassino. These new positions, often incomplete and sometimes just an indication on a map, ran from the Tyrrhenian Coast north along the Itri-Pico Road (Route 82) to Pico and then across the Liri Valley to Pontecorvo. Aerial photographs revealed that the Petrella Massif itself was not fortified and there were no German troops there—yet.

Juin reasoned that if his Goumiers could be rushed into the Aurunci to take its highest peaks by surprise they could debouch on Route 82, work in behind Pico, and the Hitler Line would become untenable. With the French behind them, the Germans would have to abandon their Gustav Line positions and the road to Rome through the Liri Valley could be forced open. But first those mountains just west of the Garigliano that the enemy already occupied had to be taken, and Juin proposed to use his regular divisions for that. He was reserving the Goums for the "impenetrable" parts of the Aurunci where the Germans were not expecting anyone.

May 11, 1944, the day scheduled for the opening of Diadem, was a quiet one on the Italian front. The Allies had kept patrol activities and routine artillery fires to a minimum, to lure the Germans into thinking that this was just another quiet day like all those of the previous few weeks. The deception had worked. The enemy figured that an Allied offensive was in the offing, but they had not expected it this early and they were totally unprepared. In fact many of their leaders were on leave in Germany and not expected back for several days.

At exactly 2300 hours, when the blanket of night permitted the Germans to be out of their fortifications and going about their routine of resupply and the strengthening of their positions, more than a thousand Allied guns suddenly roared into action. The bombardment, the heaviest of the war to date, continued throughout the night and into the following day. And when dawn broke on May 12 the Allied air forces were out doing their part to isolate the battlefield and support the ground troops.

On the ground the Allies started their advance under the cover of the artillery barrage, the British on the right, the French in the center and the Americans on the left. In the initial phase of Diadem only one of these groups met with success—the French Expeditionary Corps. To the north of the French the British were held up by fierce resistance along the Rapido, while the Polish Corps was hurled back with horrendous losses in an attempt to storm Monte Cassino. To the south the American II Corps, consisting of the green 85th and 88th Divisions in their very first action, was having a hard time getting started.

Only the French, in the center, were making progress. After hard fighting and heavy casualties they succeeded in taking

Monte Majo, the southern bastion of the Gustav Line. This, along with the capture of other hill features, opened the way into the Ausente Valley and the foothills of the Aurunci. This was the signal for the Goumiers to swing into action.

Guillaume had organized all three groups of Goums (1st, 3rd and 4th GTM) into a so-called Mountain Corps, reinforced by elements of the regular 4th Moroccan Mountain Division and the 75 mm pack howitzers of the 1st Battalion, 69th Algerian Artillery Regiment, all told about 13,000 men and 4,000 mules. They had been held in reserve on the east bank of the Garigliano where the Goumiers waited impatiently. On the morning of the 12th Guillaume gave the word and the Mountain Corps started moving out across the river. By evening the Goumiers entered Castelforte, which had already been cleansed of Germans by other French forces and continued north. A little way out of town they turned west onto a trail that led into a valley north of Monte Rotondo. Here Guillaume separated the Mountain Corps into three task forces, with the 4th GTM joined by a battalion of the 1st Tirailleurs, the 1st GTM by another battalion of the 1st Tirailleurs, while the entire 6th Moroccan Tirailleurs was attached to the 3rd GTM. The plan was for the Mountain Corps to burst out of the Ausente Valley region into the heart of the Aurunci where Allied forces were least expected, occupying the principal peaks before the Germans realized what was happening. The main targets were first Monte Petrella and then Monte Revole, neither, it was hoped, occupied by German troops.

The German theory was that when (and if) the Gustav Line was penetrated, its slowly retreating defenders would then occupy the Hitler Line, along with reinforcements from the north of Italy and from the Adriatic coast. The French plan, as visualized by Guillaume and Juin, was to take the Germans by surprise. Once in the Revole area the Goumiers would be in a position to cut Route 82, the Itri-Pico Road, and get behind the Germans at Pico. Then, when Pico and Pontecorvo had fallen, VI Corps would burst out of the Anzio beachhead, cut off the retreating Germans and join the rest of the Allies in capturing Rome.

On the night of the thirteenth, while the 3rd GTM under Colonel Bondis started north toward the key road junction of Ausonia, the 1st and 4th GTM, commanded directly by General Guillaume, moved due west toward the Petrella Massif. The long columns of men and mules, led by officers mounted on their tough little North African horses, made good progress across the valley until they came to the Ausonia Road where, late on the fourteenth, they were held up by strong enemy resistance.

To the south of the French, the Americans of the 88th Division had now found their feet and had captured the hilly area around Spigno, causing the German defenses to break up. This enabled the Goumiers to cross the road and continue on against light opposition to the foothills of the Petrella itself. Here a terrifying rock escarpment barred the way, but the Goumier's typically intuitive reconnaissance found a break just north of Spigno and by late on the morning of the fifteenth the 1st GTM had made it through and climbed the first of the challenging peaks. The 4th GTM paused at the foot of the escarpment until the 1st GTM had scouted out the surrounding terrain, and then joined it on Monte Castello. There were no Germans to be seen.

Then began one of the most remarkable forced marches in the annals of World War II, across some of the worst mountain country in Italy. The first really serious obstacle to be met was Monte Stampadura, a 4,000-foot rocky eminence of the Petrella, difficult enough to test the skills of even the most hardy Berber mountaineer. The advance guard of Goumiers, stripped of all but the lightest equipment, started up the mountainside following whatever miserable trails there were. On the afternoon of the fifteenth they reached the summit at

1600 hours, followed not too long thereafter by the rest of the group lugging the heavier armament. Still no Germans.

The columns pressed on from the Petrella at a steady pace all through the night of May 15, only halting for a brief rest every four hours. At dawn of the sixteenth the advance guard reached its objective, Monte Revole, and scrambled to its 3,800-foot crest. Once again there was no opposition; the enemy was simply unaware that thousands of savage Moroccans led by revenge-hungry Frenchmen were closing in on them.

Now it was time for the exhausted Goumiers and their mules to rest. It was also time for them to be resupplied. General Clark, just prior to the start of Diadem and not quite convinced that the Moroccans could make it over these wild mountains, had promised Guillaume an air drop of food for the men and fodder for the animals. Now thirty-six A-20s of the XII Air Force appeared in the skies over the mountains and dropped forty tons of supplies along the trails. Sixty percent of these were recovered, a remarkable record considering the difficulty of the terrain.

Having accomplished the ascent of Monte Revole, the Goumiers were now ordered to cut the vital Route 82. This would prevent the enemy from moving troops north from Itri to reinforce the all-important road junction of Pico in the Liri Valley, linchpin of the Adolf Hitler Line. Guillaume's Tabors were to move through the hills alongside the road and attack the town from the south, bringing them behind the German lines while the 3rd Algerian Division smashed into the strategically located town from the east.

On the seventeenth the Goumiers marched down the western slopes of Monte Revole in three columns. One column headed west for Monte Calvo a few miles from Revole, another turned northwest toward Monte Fagetto and the third moved in the same direction for Serra del Lago beyond Fagetto. The Germans had finally awakened to the fact that the enemy had come over the "impassable" mountains and were attacking them, and now they reacted with increasing strength.

At Monte Calvo the Goumiers met with stubborn resistance but overcame it, while the other two columns bumped into an enemy work detail building a road near Valle Piano. An advance guard of Goumiers moving cautiously through the hills warned the main body, and the Moroccans spread out silently and attacked. The Germans never had a chance as the bearded ghost-like figures in the bizarre robes descended out of the mountain mists. The record doesn't reveal the fate of the trapped workers, but one can imagine the Goumiers wiping the blood off their knives as they continued on to their destinations.

On the evening of the seventeenth the Goumiers who had reached Monte Fagetto ran into more serious trouble. Fagetto was dangerously near the defensive positions surrounding Pico, and the Germans were becoming increasingly sensitive about it. A battalion of the 15th Panzer Grenadiers accompanied by five tanks was sent to occupy Fagetto and Revole, unaware that the French were already there. The Goumiers saw them coming—and were ready. After a "don't fire until you see the whites of their eyes" order, volley after volley of rifle, machine gun and mortar fire crashed down on the unsuspecting Germans. Several of the tanks were set on fire and the rest fled back toward Pico. Those grenadiers who weren't killed were taken prisoner. Now the enemy knew for certain that the Goums had arrived.

The pack artillery that had accompanied the Tabors was also swinging into action. During that afternoon the gunners had positioned their weapons at Il Colle, adjacent to Monte Revole, and the mountain guns were able to shell the German troops moving up Route 82 from Itri. By daybeak of the eighteenth the Goumiers were well established on Monte Fagetto and nearby Monte Le Pezze where, short of supplies, they waited for more pack trains to come up. By the nineteenth, their supply difficulties solved, they had occupied the town of Campodimele. Here they were held up by German self-propelled guns on the highway, but Campodimele was to become a rallying point for the Mountain Corps.

By now Guillaume had sent strong patrols across Route 82 into the German occupied mountains on the other side. One such patrol crossed the highway and scaled Monte Vele, silencing what few of its surprised defenders it ran across. The patrol had brought with it artillery forward observers who radioed fire directions to the mountain battery on Il Colle, which kept up a steady and very accurate fire on Route 82. The patrol spent all of the nineteenth behind the enemy lines directing the artillery, then slipped silently down the mountainside and back across the highway. It even brought back with it a handful of crestfallen prisoners.

On the eastern side of the road French troops now occupied the mountains from Monte Calvo to Campodimele. Other French forces, including Colonel Bondis' task force of Goumiers and Tirailleurs, which had separated from Guillaume's column as they left the Ausente Valley, had come up through the mountains north of Guillaume, and positioned themselves east of Pico. The French were now ready to attack that hub of the Hitler Line from two directions.

To see how the Bondis task force had reached that position, let's go back to May 12. As the Bondis group split from the main body of the Mountain Corps, it too faced supposedly impassable mountain barriers. But first it had to cross the Ausente Valley, occupied here and there by German units, while the regular FEC divisions cleaned up the mountainous regions around Monte Majo, just west of the Garigliano. The Goumiers passed south of Ausonia where German troops were still holding out against the 3rd Algerian Division and continued right up to the foothills of their first major objective, Monte Fammera. Here they were stymied by an unscalable escarpment, but once again the Goumiers' innate mountaineering instincts came into play. A mounted reconnaissance platoon, scouting along the base of the rocky barrier, found a small opening southwest of Ausonia and scrambled up a narrow defile to the top. It was after dark of the sixteenth before the entire Bondis group, now joined by the 6th Moroccan Tirailleurs, managed to make its way through the break and up into the mountain. The task force continued on, making short work of the 171st Field Replacement Battalion, the only enemy force that tried to bar its way.

In the meanwhile, Ausonia had fallen to the Algerians who had now moved up to besiege Esperia. While they attacked from the east the Goumiers positioned in the hills to the southwest threatened to swing around and swoop down on the town from the rear. The Germans didn't wait. Threatened with encirclement, they pulled out of Esperia on the 17th, leaving this strategic village to the French.

The Bondis task force continued on from Monte Fammera against heavy opposition to a point in the mountains south of Monte Del Lago and then turned north to the peaks overlooking Sant'Oliva. The Germans had now become fully aware of the extent of the French penetration and were bringing in strong reinforcements, including the crack 26th Panzer Division, to stop the drive on Pico.

As we have seen, by May 19 there was now a French line anchored on the left by Guillaume's Mountain Corps at Monte Calvo and Campodimele. In the center, just north of Campodimele, the rest of the Mountain Corps under Colonel Bondis was positioned through the hills to a point just south of Sant'Oliva. From there the line was held by the 1st Motorized Infantry Division, heavily engaged along the south bank of the Liri.

This was not exactly according to plan, as the British Eighth Army was supposed to be advancing through the Liri Valley in line with the FEC. However the British were at first held up along the Rapido and at Monte Cassino by fierce enemy opposition, and then by the many streams that criss-crossed the valley, even in the dry season. Then, too, they were overmechanized for the terrain. Their huge amount of motor transport caused unbelievable traffic snarls on the inadequate road net, and now they were six miles behind the mule-transported French. This left the right flank of the FEC exposed and the German guns on the north side of the Liri were taking their toll.

Orders were given for the 3rd Algerian Division to attack Pico from the east while the Tabors were to advance from the south. To the Germans Pico was of the utmost importance, and the 26th Panzer Division was called upon to hold it at all costs, giving the shattered remnants of the German units south of the Liri a chance to escape to the next line of defenses in the hills just below Rome.

As the Algerians closed in on Pico, the 4th GTM, directly under Guillaume, and Bondis' 3rd GTM moved north through the hill country alongside Route 82 toward Pico, putting additional pressure on the defenders. The American 756th Tank Battalion was now attached to the French and the Goumiers enjoyed riding on the tanks. It was a new experience for the Berber mountaineers, and they embraced it with childish delight.

Another task force of Goumiers, the 1st GTM under Colonel Paul Cherrière, had been detached from the main body. It crossed Route 82 and was making its way through the hills on the west side of the highway, with the mission of holding off any possible enemy attacks from that direction. But it was now ordered to rejoin the Guillaume group as the Mountain Corps neared Pico. Then orders were changed again, and it was the Guillaume group's turn to cross Route 82 and head west for Lenola while Cherrière's people continued on toward Pico.

To the east of Pico the battle had been raging for two days with the Germans going all out. They had brought up dozens of tanks, including the huge Tigers, in addition to six-barrelled Nebelwerfers (the frightening "screaming meemies") and the famous 88s, against the Algerians and the 1st Motorized. There were heavy casualties on both sides, but on the 22nd scouts of the 7th Algerian Tirailleurs reported that the Germans were evacuating the town. That morning the Algerians entered Pico from the east while the Moroccans of the Cherrière force came in from the south. The two groups continued mopping up operations and by late afternoon Pico was entirely in Allied hands.

In the meanwhile Guillaume's force that had been diverted west into the mountains toward Lenola was beginning to meet heavy resistance. The Goumiers took the heights south and east of the town and ran into elements of the American II Corps coming up on their left flank. American armor still operating on Route 82 aided the Mountain Corps by knocking out enemy self-propelled guns on the Lenola-Pico Road, enabling Guillaume's men to gain the heights north of Lenola. With the town surrounded, its garrison of what was left of a battalion of the 276th Grenadier Regiment surrendered, and 250 more Germans became POWs.

While many German units were still fighting stubbornly, the French were now behind the Adolf Hitler Line in numbers. On May 23 the VI Corps started pushing out of the Anzio beachhead, and the Eighth Army attacked through what was left of the German defenses in the Liri Valley. In concert with these drives the FEC renewed its attack in the mountains west of Route 82, with the Goumiers pushing toward Castro dei Volsci and Amaseno. Fresh enemy troops drawn in desperation from as far away as the Adriatic regions were thrown against them and although the 1st GTM gained the heights of Monte Pizzuto the Germans counterattacked and pushed the Goumiers off. It was fortunate that the French had maintained close contact with II Corps, for troops of the 88th Division came up from Monte Monsicardi and helped Guillaume's men to regain the mountaintop. American corps artillery also aided the Mountain Corps in the battle for Villecorsa, which was a hub of local German resistance and American tanks were vital in the street battles that ended in the eventual capture of that town.

Now the German forces were collapsing everywhere and the pursuit turned into a rout. The mobility of the Goumiers in the mountains was a prime factor in enabling the French troops to move from peak to peak of the Lepini range, winkling out the rear guards and adding to the prisoner bag. Resistance at this stage was spotty. Sometimes the remnants of the better German units fought hard and died in their dugouts while others such as those outfits made up of Russian POWs, "volunteers" from the eastern front, gave up without a struggle, just glad to be alive.

Finally descending the western slopes of the Lepinis, the French ended up on Route 6, one of the main highways into Rome. Here they were ordered to clear the road to make way for the Eighth Army coming up behind them in the Liri Valley. At this time there was considerable argument at higher levels as to which of the Allied troops would actually enter Rome. It was finally decided that the Fifth Army should have that honor and General Clark named II Corps for the job. This was a disappointment to Juin since his FEC had done so much of the bitter mountain fighting that led to the Eternal City's liberation. He did, however, accompany General Clark into the Italian capital (as did the other corps commanders) while his troops continued chasing the Germans across the Aniene River east of Rome.

While the FEC missed the thrill of the tumultuous welcome given the Allied troops who fought their way into the city, it was probably just as well for the Goumiers. They were not popular with the Italians. This was the result of the off-duty conduct of some of them in the mountain villages and isolated valley farms they passed through along the way. In truth, certain elements among the Moroccans had engaged in a wild spree of rape and pillage across the Italian countryside when they were not busy killing Germans.

Not that they had anything against the Italians. (For that matter, they had nothing against the Germans.) Their origins, however, cannot be forgotten; to the Moroccan tribesman, that was the way war was waged. To the victor belonged the spoils, and the Goumiers were somewhat puzzled by the restraints put upon them by their officers. The French had long realized the propensity of their irregular troops for irregular conduct. Only a few years before, General Giraud had tried to justify the brutal means used by the French in putting down the very tribes from which the Tabors had later been recruited. At that time he told a reporter that these mountain people "lived only for brigandage and war. It would be impossible for the French to develop the country so long as they remained in their mountain fastnesses, capable of swooping down on the peaceful farmers of the plain."[9]

Now, as the opportunity presented itself, these basic instincts rose to the fore. Reports came in to Fifth Army headquarters of women of all ages being violated, of livestock being driven off, of household goods looted and money stolen and even of murder. Clark was appalled. He contacted Juin who immediately ordered that the offenders be caught and summarily punished. The Tabor officers freely admitted that in some cases they had lost control of their men, and instantly went about correcting the situation. Where there was no doubt of guilt, those offenders were shot out of hand, while hastily convened courts martial decided the fate of others. In the end it was officially reported that "about" fifteen Moroccans had been executed "in the field" while fifty-four others were sentenced to anywhere from five years imprisonment to life for murder, attempted murder, rape, attempted rape or theft.[10]

These crimes tarnished the honor of the French army in Italy and horrified Juin and the rest of the French command.

General Guillaume, as Commandant of the Moroccan Tabors, was particularly affected. Although the indignation caused by the acts of his men gradually died down, the subject would come back to haunt him later. Meanwhile, the authorities decided they might be able to cool the carnal ardor of the Goumiers by importing Berber women, and American 1st's were soon loaded with North African ladies bound for the rear area camps of the Tabors.[11] The depredations ceased, but the disgrace lingered on.

The liberation of Rome did not end the martial activities of the Goums in Italy. Although the French knew they would soon be leaving the Fifth Army to take part in Operation Dragoon, the invasion of southern France, there were still Germans to fight here and now. The order had been given to push on, keeping the retreating remnants of the German army off balance. The object of the Germans was to reach the already prepared field fortifications of the so-called Gothic Line, strung across northern Italy, south of Bologna. Here they hoped to hold off the Allies for another winter, until Hitler's "secret weapons" were ready to win the war for them.

The Germans moved north as fast as they could, at various points leaving behind a rear guard of a few tanks, self-propelled guns or truck-borne infantry to hold up their pursuers. Then, when the opposition became too hot, they would take off at high speed, leaving the Allied troops in the dust. All the time, of course, they were harried by the Allied air forces, but they still managed to move on. The problem for the pursuers was that the ports in Allied hands were now left far behind and all supplies had to be hauled long distances by truck. That left few vehicles for the pursuing infantry and much of the chase had to be carried on by troops on foot, marching along the dusty roads at the same pace as their quarry.

The chase slowed down as the Germans became better organized and resistance stiffened. To meet this challenge Juin put together the 3rd Algerian Division and the 1st Motorized Division to form a *Groupe de Chasse*, a pursuit group under General Edgard de Larminat, with Guillaume's Tabors and Moroccan Tirailleurs taking over the French left flank. The axis of the advance was up a main highway, Route 2, which put Guillaume's group in contact with the right flank of the newly formed American IV Corps moving up the coast along Route 1.

On June 20 the French were stopped cold by the strongest enemy defenses met by Allied troops anywhere since Rome. The Germans were well dug in, forming a line south of the Orcia River, with the strongest part covering the easily fordable crossings. The defenders were up to their old tricks, with rifle pits, machine gun nests, mines, wire and, worst of all, more well-placed artillery than had been seen in many weeks. The defending troops were amongst the best they had left, including the 4th Parachute Division, the 356th Grenadier Division and elements of the 20th GAF (German Air Force) Field Division, the 26th Panzer Division and the 29th Panzer Grenadier Division.[12]

Facing these units were the 3rd Algerian and 2nd Moroccan Divisions, the latter replacing the 1st Motorized, which had been pulled out of the line to prepare for the southern France invasion, and the Goums. After two days of heavy fighting with very little progress, Juin, a man who never believed in beating his head against the wall, decided to try a flanking movement. He sent Guillaume's force to ford the Ombrone, a winding extension of the Orcia, and move around behind the German lines. Joined by the armored cars of the 4th Moroccan Spahis and maintaining contact with the American 1st Armored Division on the left, the Tabors crossed the Ombrone and advanced northeast along the west bank of the river. This move threatened the German rear and unhinged the enemy line. On the twenty-fifth the Moroccan Tirailleurs of the 2nd Division broke through the enemy positions and crossed the Orcia, followed the next day by the Algerians. After more heavy fighting the pursuit resumed, periodically delayed by the usual rear guard actions, demolitions, mines and booby traps.

This was to be the last major action of the Goums in Italy. On July 3 they marched into the ancient town of Siena which had been evacuated by the Germans as the Moroccans approached. The Tabors were soon relieved of all combat duties and eventually sent to Naples where they joined the other French troops preparing for Operation Dragoon. But were they actually to take part in the invasion of the southern coast of France? There seemed to be some doubt about that.

In the meanwhile Colonel Boyer de Latour's 2nd *Groupe de Tabors Marocains,* languishing in Corsica and spoiling for a fight, finally got its chance for another crack at the Germans. Allied Force Headquarters decided that it was time to take out the island of Elba, famous scene of Napoleon's first exile. It was dangerously near the coast of Italy, off Piombino on the flank of the Allied advance. The operation had originally been planned to coincide with the beginning of Diadem, but lack of sufficient aircraft for cover caused postponement to mid-June.

Elba was directly across the Tyrrhenian Sea from the port of Bastia in Corsica (on a clear day it could be seen from there) so that was a logical embarkation point for the assault. The German-held island had been used as an emergency landing field for damaged or out-of-fuel Luftwaffe aircraft and as a home base for raiding German E-Boats. It had a formidable garrison that was expected to resist fanatically. The officers of the Tabors had been looking at it through their field glasses for months and licking their lips. Now, at last. . . .

Chosen as the main force for the attack was the 9th Colonial Division of Sengalese troops, reinforced by commandos of the Shock Battalion and de Latour's Goumiers. The entire expedition was to be commanded by General Henry Martin under the overall supervision of General Jean de Lattre de Tassigny as a rehearsal for the landing in southern France.

The Goumiers landed on Elba in what was designated "Operation Brassard" on June 17, and after two days of hard fighting the French had completely defeated the garrison. The cost was high, more than 1,000 casualties, but the rewards were considerable: security of the left flank of the Fifth Army in Italy and 1,800[13] German prisoners. It was also excellent training for staff and troops for the proposed assault on southern France. And the Goumiers of the 2nd GTM had gotten their wish for more action. Aside from the casualties, there was one other downside; there were reports of extensive looting by the French forces.[14]

The Italian campaign was the supreme testing ground for the Moroccan Tabors. Could these lightly armed primitive tribesmen survive in modern warfare? Their officers maintained that they could and did, that their performance in the mountains of Italy was proof of their value, even in the most difficult circumstances. Certainly their remarkable exploits in the first eight days of Diadem was strong evidence that this was true. The spectacular thrust of some 13,000 men through the trackless Aurunci to cut the Itri-Pico Road behind the Hitler Line was a matchless feat that probably could not have been equalled by any other troops then in Italy. Supply alone, with one air drop and 4,000 mules, was in itself an almost magical accomplishment.

These spectacular acts were a reflection of the exceptional abilities of the French officers. Here were serious professionals, determined to redress the disgrace of the French army in its capitulation to Hitler's forces in Europe. Many were more experienced than some of their Allies, having only recently been engaged in France's colonial wars, particularly in the twenty-two years of the Moroccan pacification with its emphasis on mountain warfare.

Then, too, the French were used to handling native troops, especially North Africans. As we have seen, the commander of all French forces was *Giraud l'Africain*, while Juin, commander of the French Expeditionary Corps in Italy, was himself a North African, a *pied noir* from Bone in Algeria who had commanded Arabs and Berbers much of his life. Juin was also a brilliant tactician, and the prime advocate of the FEC's route through the mountains toward Rome, declaring that he would much rather go through the mountains than across the more level terrain where the Germans can better site their automatic weapons and artillery and can use their tanks. And he strongly supported Guillaume and his Goumiers as practitioners of that theory.[15]

Guillaume himself, although by that time a Brigadier General, was very much an "up front" officer, conducting personal reconnaissances, scrambling through the rocky mountain trails on horseback and often under fire as he urged his Goumiers forward with the Berber cry, "*Zidou l'goudem*!"[16]

The Allied high command, although at first reluctant to listen to their advice, eventually respected the knowledge of the senior French officers and the extraordinary ability of their troops in the mountains. Both Alexander and Clark were devastated by the loss of the FEC when it was relieved of duty with the Fifth Army in July 1944. Clark particularly missed Juin, and in his memoirs the American general wrote of him, "No finer soldier ever lived."[17]

Even the Germans admired the French troops in Italy. General Albert Kesselring, the overall commander of German forces there reported, "British and American tactics were again [too] methodical. Local successes were seldom exploited. On the other hand the French, particularly the Moroccans, fought with great élan, and exploited each local success by concentrating immediately all available forces at the weakened point."

General Fritz Wentzell, the German Tenth Army's chief of staff, echoed his superior's sentiments. When the German high command demanded to know why the army's defenses were crumbling so fast, Wentzell replied, "You don't know the French colonial troops. They are a fierce bunch. Life means nothing to them."[18]

The British, too, added their praise of the Goumiers' accomplishments. Fred Majdalany, prominent author of World War II historic themes, wrote:

> The *goumiers* are hawk-faced Moroccan troops whose specialty is mountain fighting. Their especial value is their uncanny gift for moving silently through trackless mountain country. Their method of working is similar to the action of an incoming tide on a series of sand castles. These waves of *goums* could be unloosed on a shapeless mass of mountain country that orthodox troops would find impassable. They would move up silently on any opposition that presented itself, dispose of it and push on regardless of what was happening to those on their right or left. They had a habit of bringing back evidence of the number of victims they had killed, which made them an unpleasant enemy to face.[19]

In the widely seen British television documentary *The World at War*, the work of the Tabors was also lauded. A British officer commented that after Diadem the Goums were held in awe, and British troops would often refer to any particularly audacious attack as "gouming it."

At the conclusion of the French service in Italy, when all units were withdrawn from the Fifth Army to prepare for Dragoon, a report was made by the French inspector general's department on the strengths and weaknesses of the Goumiers' contribution. It was agreed that the Moroccan irregulars were superb at scouting and patrolling, especially in mountain areas too difficult for regular troops. In the attack, particularly if it was not against long-prepared defenses, they were expert at what the French called *débordement*, which translates as "overflowing," but which might better be interpreted as "swarming." This was the swift mass attack that took the enemy by surprise and overwhelmed him even before he knew what was happening.

They were also found to be very good at cleaning out pockets of resistance that had been by-passed by regular units, and at locating and taking prisoner enemy stragglers, no matter how well they tried to hide themselves. And of course their hard

Goumiers in North Africa.

marching and legendary endurance under the worst possible conditions was duly noted, as were their cleverness at ambushes and their skill at dirty tricks.

So much for their strong points. The Goums' major deficiency seemed to be a lack of initiative when their French leaders were *hors de combat.* Whenever the officers were put out of action by death or wounds the efficiency of the Goumiers suffered noticeably. Another weakness was a certain hesitancy in attacking well-prepared field fortifications of the type so often met within the Italian campaign. The tribesmen preferred a war of movement to a sedentary siege, which took too much time and patience. They seemed also to be more affected by heavy artillery fire and the ever present mines and booby traps than were the regular troops. And they didn't like tanks—not surprising since they had no organic artillery or antitank guns of their own.[20]

Guillaume took these criticisms in stride and agreed with many of them. With the coming return to France in mind he sent a report to Juin outlining how the deficiencies could be corrected. Additional French cadres were uppermost in his thoughts, but he had other suggestions as well. Since in Italy the horsed reconnaissance platoons had been found to be exceptionally vulnerable to enemy fire, he thought the mounted units should be reduced in size, but not eliminated. Conversely, he wanted a small increase in the number of motor vehicles, useful for administrative purposes when the Goums, as they sometimes did, came down out of the mountains. More importantly, he urged that the Tabors be equipped with antitank guns of the type provided to Allied airborne troops. He wrote:

> The Moroccan Goums have shown on the Italian front their aptitude for combat in Europe if they are employed under a qualified command [meaning himself] and used in a terrain and with a mission corresponding to

> their particular abilities. Organized above all as a light mountain infantry with the obvious advantage of mobility over that of regular infantry, they are excellent in the exploitation of success in mountainous regions.

Then, obviously fearful that the Goums might not be included in Operation Dragoon, Guillaume went into a passionate defense of their right to take part. He continued:

> For the success they have won in Tunisia, in Sicily, in Corsica, in Italy, for their sacrifices in all theatres of operation, the Moroccan Goums have the right to claim the honor of pursuing the struggle on the sacred soil of France with the view of hastening the liberation of our country.
>
> In this final phase of the war it would be inconceivable to leave unemployed those units which have the ability in difficult terrain to supplement the tanks and motorized formations less able to fight in the many mountainous regions of Europe.[21]

Guillaume concluded his message by calling attention to what was probably the principal reason for AFHQ's hesitation to use the Goums in France—the rape and pillage attributed to the Goumiers in Italy. In this matter he took a strange stance. Although the fact that the Goumiers were guilty was generally acknowledged by all (and for which many had already been punished), Guillaume suggested the authorization of a board of inquiry to determine the identity of the *real* culprits. He then suggested that the guilty parties were actually rear area service troops, or perhaps the Tirailleurs, or maybe gangs of deserters—anyone but his Goumiers. But, he predicted, all that would change with a substantial increase in French cadres who would then be able to maintain the strictest discipline in the

Tabors. In other words, the Goumiers didn't do it—but they won't do it again.

There was an air of hysteria in this last suggestion of innocence. Obviously, General Guillaume wanted to lead his Goumiers into France in the worst possible way, and he thought Juin could help him do it. Perhaps he could, for Juin's next assignment was as Chief of Staff of National Defense, a promotion that put him very close to de Gaulle himself. But of more immediate importance to Guillaume would be the man selected to become the commanding officer of the newly formed First French Army and the leader of all French forces in Operation Dragoon, General Jean de Lattre de Tassigny.

CHAPTER 4

At Last—France

On August 16, 1944, the second wave of a massive Allied fleet approached the coast of southern France. Assembled on the deck of the former Polish liner *Batory* was the vanguard of Army B, the French force coming to join in the liberation of their homeland. Many of those on board hadn't seen their native land since it was occupied by the hated Germans years before, while others had escaped to join the Allied armies only recently. But to all of them it was a heart-stopping moment.

As the shoreline came into view across the calm sunlit waters, someone started to sing the "Marseillaise." Others immediately joined in and soon all along the Mediterranean shore it seemed that every Frenchman on every ship was bellowing the stirring words.[1] It was like the scene from the film *Casablanca*—only this time it was for real.

Among the singers was the commander of the French invasion forces, General Jean de Lattre de Tassigny. Unlike Giraud, Juin, Guillaume and so many other senior French officers in World War II, de Lattre was not an *Africain*. He had not patrolled the desert sands of the Sahara nor fought dissident tribesmen in the Moroccan mountains. He was, however, quite literally a *beau sabreur*; his body bore the scars of sabre wounds he received in the 1914 war when, as a young lieutenant of cavalry, he fought hand-to-hand with a German Uhlan officer.[2] De Lattre was, in short, a soldier, and he recognized fighters when he saw them, even if they were a bit strange looking. In spite of his limited experience in North Africa (he had served a short while in prewar Tunisia) he had heard about and appreciated the fighting abilities of the Goums.

His first actual command of Moroccan tribesmen, however, was not until the previous June when de Latour's 2nd GTM was a part of the expeditionary force that conquered the island of Elba. It was then, as overall commander of the expedition, that de Lattre learned first hand just how good they could be—and not in their regular role as mountain fighters either, but rather in their first amphibious operation. When he saw them in action the general was thinking ahead to southern France.

Planning for Elba had been an on-again, off-again affair, and de Lattre was right in the middle of it. The attack was first scheduled to start at the same time as Diadem, but was postponed for lack of available air cover. Then it was revitalized with the object of protecting the flank of the Fifth Army as it progressed up the Italian coast. And when the Allied drive was held up some miles below Piombino, it was called off again. Finally, much to de Lattre's relief, the date was definitely set with the approval of higher headquarters for June 17. This time it was to be a rehearsal for Dragoon, for it was now discovered that the coastline of Elba was similar to that of Provence.

The Germans knew that a landing on Elba was coming, for that entire Mediterranean area was infested with spies and line-crossers. They just didn't know when or at what point the blow would fall. Hitler had, as usual, given the word: Don't give an inch, fight to the last man. And General Gall, the commander on Elba, was preparing to do just that.

As soon as he realized an attack was imminent, Gall went to work to upgrade the defenses of his island with concrete, wire, mines, booby traps and, most deadly of all, strategically placed artillery, some sixty medium and heavy pieces. The terrain itself was excellent for defense. The island, of irregular shape, was more than twenty miles long with a mountainous spine down the center with peaks over 3,000-feet high. The coastline was mostly steep cliffs with just a few horseshoe shaped bays with enough beaches to make a landing for a sizable force possible.

The assault was to be made from nearby Corsica where the main attacking force was waiting to embark. It consisted of two regimental combat teams of the untried 9th Colonial Infantry Division, West Africans with French officers, and Boyer de Latour's seasoned 2nd GTM, which had been impatiently marking time in Corsica for nearly a year. There were also a number of commando units, including elements of the French *Bataillon de Choc*, the African Commando and the British Royal Marines, all of whom were scheduled to land the night before the main force and take out as many of the guns as they could.

The naval arrangements for the assault were under command of the British Admiral Troubridge, while the air cover was provided by the Americans under Colonel Darcy. There were 270 vessels of all sizes and types, British and French, that left the Corsican ports of Bastia and Porto Vecchio in broad daylight on July 15 and headed due south in an attempt to fool the enemy as to their destination. Then, under cover of darkness, they turned northeast to land the commandos on various parts of Elba. Fierce fighting broke out all over the island and continued throughout the next day as the commandos silenced many of the German batteries.

But few things in warfare ever turn out exactly as expected—for either side. General Gall had expected the main assault to fall on Porto Ferraio, Elba's principal town and port, on the north side of the island. Instead, the French had selected the beaches of Marino di Campo on the south coast for the landings of the Tabors and Colonials. The main attack started on the seventeenth.

Gall, surprised, reacted quickly. With that characteristic German ability to change plans without missing a beat, he hurriedly strengthened his defenses at Marino di Campo. There was heavy fighting, but the French soon realized that their planned attack at that point was going to be too costly, and they withdrew.

The Germans, however, had no monopoly on quick adjustments of plan. The French command lost no time in finding an alternate landing place across the bay from Marino di Campo. It was a small cove near a town called Nercio, and although the beaches were not large enough for heavy equipment or artillery, the Goumiers managed to land under cover of a naval smoke screen and infiltrate into the interior of the island. They then advanced along the south shore to pierce the defenses of Porto Longone on the east end, after which Lieutenant-Colonel Edom turned his 6th Tabor north to overrun the Isthmus of Puccio.

By this time there were French colonials, commandos and Goumiers throughout Elba, and after two days of fighting it was all over. The Germans, who had thought their island impregnable, surrendered and the tricolor flew over what had been the exiled Napoleon's quarters in 1814.

With the exception that General Gall had escaped by submarine to Italy, the Elba affair was a thoroughgoing victory for the Allies and a perfect example of inter-Allied cooperation. De Lattre got along famously with Troubridge and Darcy, and everyone was happy except the Germans. It was also an interesting naval victory; the British considered it equal in terms of difficulty and eventual success to any other amphibious operation in the Mediterranean up to that time.

To the Goums it was one more example of their adaptability, proof that they were not just mountain soldiers. De Lattre was impressed and definitely wanted them for Dragoon. Getting them on the troop list for France, however, would not be easy, but in that connection de Lattre would be their savior. Without his influence and his tactful handling of higher headquarters, the Tabors would have probably been sent back to Africa to their security duties in the Atlas. For in spite of their now-proven abilities, the tales of rape and pillage persisted and became worse with each retelling. The horror stories had even come to the attention of the Vatican, and Pope Pius XII had personally objected to the further use of the tribesmen in Europe.

But even without their tarnished reputation, approving the Goums for Operation Dragoon would have been a hard sell. Dragoon was a huge operation eventually entailing five battleships, nine escort carriers with 216 aircraft, 122 destroyers and escort vessels and 466 landing craft, all from five navies—American, British, French, Australian and Greek[3]—and an imposing fleet of transports and supply ships as well. Shipping space was necessarily tight, and the prospect of providing room for thousands of these primitive tribesmen, to say nothing of the particular problems of loading and unloading their mules and horses, did not appeal to the staff of Force 163, the planning unit responsible. There was much grousing and nay-saying at the conference tables, and not a few American and British planning officers still had reservations about even the most modern and well-equipped (by the Americans) of French forces, to say nothing of these wild men from the North African mountains. There were many very serious objections to their inclusion in the invasion forces.

General Alexander Patch, the American officer in charge of the landings in southern France, was not sympathetic and he was not convinced. Nor did the naval authorities on the planning staff like the idea of the Goumiers' mules dirtying their nice neat ships.

But de Lattre was nothing if not persuasive. He pointed out the difficulties of the mountainous terrain surrounding Toulon and Marseilles, the principal ports and the main objectives of the initial French landings. They would need trained mountain troops and the Goums were the best there were. Hadn't they proved as much in Tunisia, Sicily and Italy? Moreover, there were serious mountains in the path of the Allied armies after the landings—the Vosges stood squarely across the routes to Alsace, the Rhine and Germany, and the French Alps, too, had to be defended.

De Lattre's logic and persistence finally overcame the objections, and it was agreed to accept a force of Goumiers and a group of mountain artillery[4] to land on the beaches starting D-Day plus two. At this stage the numbers were left vague. De Lattre, knowing how these things worked, told his staff, "We speak of 1,000, we think of 2,000, and we embark 6,000."[5] Guillaume was elated and the preparation of the Tabors was intensified.

But then the old difficulties arose again. On June 30, even while the Goumiers were approaching Siena in their last action in Italy, the purported depredations of the Goumiers in the advance on Rome came up once more. In an audience granted to General de Gaulle, the pope again complained about the rape and pillage public rumor attributed to the Moroccans. And once again, as a result of this discussion, their proposed participation in Dragoon was cancelled.

When he was informed of this, Guillaume hit the roof. He stormed through the corridors of power in Algiers, trying to have this latest order retracted. A better frontline fighter than a diplomat, he was unsuccessful in his efforts.

Now de Lattre took over. On July 18 he wrote a flowery letter to de Gaulle, "General Béthouart has told me of your unfavorable opinion of the projected participation of the Moroccan Goums in the first phase of Operation Anvil [Dragoon]. I cannot imagine that the employment of the Goums in this fashion could be contrary to your wishes in any way."

He then went on to point out the particular value of the Goums and their special skills in the formidable mountains of Europe. He further argued that the shipping tables were already made up and any change, if not already impossible at this stage, could not be made without "serious inconvenience."

He added as a clincher, "I further assure you with the most extreme vigor, that any incident of the reproachful nature that occurred in Italy will not occur under the sun of France."[6]

The letter did the trick. De Gaulle relented and the Goums were once more on the shipping list for the early stages of Dragoon. The only proviso was that in future battles the Goumiers were not to be used within cities or large towns. It was one more example of de Lattre's knack for getting things done, and Guillaume and his Tabors were fortunate in having this able man in high command take such an interest in them.

Jean de Lattre was indeed a complex character and seemed to be different things to different people. His relationship to his American superior, General Patch, has been described as being similar to that of Patton to Eisenhower. De Lattre was

> impulsive, headstrong, prone to interpret orders to suit his own needs, and eager to avenge the humiliation France had suffered at the hands of the Germans. In short, he was difficult to handle. Fortunately, both he and Patch quickly developed a mutual respect for each other. The task was made easier by Patch's understanding of how anxious the French were to free their homeland. Thus he allowed de Lattre to take liberties that normally would be denied to other commanders. The Frenchman responded by providing victories in the field.[7]

Perhaps a more balanced view of de Lattre's talents would come from Charles de Gaulle's postwar writings. "De Lattre, emotional, flexible, farsighted and widely curious, influencing the minds around him by the ardor of his spirit and winning loyalty by the exertions of his soul, heading toward his goal by sudden and unexpected leaps, although often well calculated ones."[8]

Whether or not the "exertions of his soul" won the loyalty of Guillaume, something about him certainly did, for from then on the Goums were totally de Lattre's men. His calm restored by the news that his Tabors would definitely land in France, Guillaume set about making his plans for the coming invasion. After being pulled out of the line, the three GTM's in Italy were sent down to the Naples area where it was decided that the 4th Group, which had been in combat the longest, would be sent back to North Africa for rest and the less arduous security duty. (It would be brought back to Europe later.) Back in Africa it would replace four Tabors that had been kept there to supply replacements for the 1st and 3rd GTMs, then undergoing amphibious training in southern Italy, and the 2nd, still in Corsica.

The 1st and 3rd Groups finally joined their comrades in Corsica, and as the great day grew near they were definitely scheduled for an early phase of the landings on the beaches of southern France. Thanks in large part to the efforts of Brigadier-General John P. Ratay, chief of the American base in Corsica and an old friend of Morocco, they would be assured of their desired place in the invasion.[9] The Goums would be 6,000 strong (as predicted by de Lattre), with 1,200 mules to dirty up the nice clean ships.

The plan was for the American Seventh Army of three infantry divisions reinforced by Combat Command "Sudre" (CC1) of the 1st French Armored Division and French Commandos to land on the beaches of Provence on D-Day, while a huge airborne army dropped some ten miles inland to trap as many retreating Germans as they could and to foil any possible attack from the Italian Alps. Then, in the second echelon would come French provisional "Army B" consisting of the rest of the 1st Armored Division (du Vigier), the 9th Colonial Division (Magnan), the 3rd Algerian Division (de Monsabert), the 1st Free French Division (Brosset)—and, of course, Guillaume's

Tabors. Their job was to take the vital port cities of Toulon and Marseilles, for their Allies agreed that the French forces should have that important honor. There were serious supply difficulties throughout the Allied command in France, and the ports were badly needed.

The German defenders of southern France were troops of the Nineteenth Army under the able and determined General Friedrich Wiese, but his forces were weakened by the continuing loss of some of his best troops, withdrawn to help defend equally threatened positions in other parts of France. The troops left in the two major cities were the excellent 242nd Infantry Division and the Kriegsmarine (German navy, with most of its personnel converted to infantry) in Toulon, and the equally capable 244th Infantry Division, plus naval and Luftwaffe ground units in and around Marseille. The German navy itself consisted only of small surface craft and a few U-boats, while the Luftwaffe in the south of France had scarcely 200 planes left.

On D-Day, August 15, 1944, in the early morning hours, 10,000 American and British paratroopers of the 1st Airborne Task Force dropped into southern France some ten miles inland from the Mediterranean shores. It was the most successful airborne operation yet, with 60 percent of its people landing on target. They met comparatively little opposition. Landing on the beaches later in the morning, the infantry and armor of the Seventh Army were equally successful.

The next day de Lattre started landing his "Army B" on the beaches of Provence—and was immediately faced with a dilemma. His quick mind had come up with a new idea. Should he attack Toulon at once or, as planned, wait for more reinforcements to land? He decided on the bolder plan, to hit the city without waiting.

With Patch's permission, French troops attacked through the mountains and were soon fighting in the heart of the city.

Under the usual Hitler order to fight to the last man, the German soldiers and sailors defended Fort Coudon and the ammunition magazine in Toulon with desperate courage and were only overcome with the help of flame throwers, tank destroyers and artillery. And they were still fighting when de Lattre had another bold idea.

The general had previously sent out Colonel Bonjour's Spahis in their armored cars to scout along the main route between Toulon and Marseilles. On the nineteenth they reported back that they had reached and captured the crossroads of Le Camp, almost halfway to Marseilles, without meeting any heavy German opposition. This set de Lattre's mind racing ahead, and he had this latest brainstorm: Since they were so much nearer to Marseilles than they expected to be at this time, why not launch the planned attack on that even more important port *right away*?

But there were serious downsides to this idea. He was still dangerously short of troops, even though the original French landing had been quick and efficient and ahead of schedule. (The transports, after unloading, had promptly turned around and gone back to Corsica to pick up another echelon of de Lattre's troops, including the remainder of the 3rd DIA, the Tabors and the Shock Battalion, and these had already landed.) But most of his available troops were still fighting a desperate battle with last-ditch Germans in Toulon. And some of his force had not yet even embarked from their initial ports.

So de Lattre had an agonizing decision to make. After considerable thought he took one of his "sudden and unexpected leaps." He just couldn't resist the temptation—he decided to order the attack on Marseilles without delay.

Patch's staff thought the idea even crazier than the premature attack on Toulon, particularly since the fighting was still going on there and the Germans in that city had not yet surrendered. The original plan had called for the attack on Marseilles to commence only *after* Toulon had been mopped up. But Patch, an aggressive fighter like de Lattre, approved the new idea, and the Frenchman lost no time in putting his troops on the move. Leaving the 1st DFL and the Senegalese Tirailleurs of the 9th DIC to finish the job in Toulon, he ordered elements of the 1st Armored Division, part of the 3rd Algerian Division and the Goums to head for Marseilles—all under command of de Monsabert.

Marseilles was a big city, the second largest in France, and the Germans had turned it into a fortress. Its suburbs and approaches were widespread and equally well fortified. Four main roads led into this metropolis, all blocked by German strongholds with the usual machine guns, mines and wire and sometimes artillery. There were some 150 to 200 guns of 75 mm to 220 mm in and around the city, and there were heavy coastal defense guns on the outlying islands that could be turned around to shell any attacks from the land side. It was not a continuous line, but every possible concrete or stone building, factory, warehouse or quarry in this heavily industrialized region had become a battlement, with its defenders ready to die for the Fuehrer.

The attacking force consisted of Sudre's CCI of the 1st Armored Division, Chappuis' 7th RTA of the 3rd DIA and all three groups of Guillaume's Tabors. The tanks led the way. After a brief fight they pushed past Cuges-les-Pins and crushed a casement blocking the Col de l'Ange (Angel Pass). By nightfall of the twentieth they had reached Aubagne, the first of the heavily fortified villages barring the road to Marseilles.

The Tabors were on the way behind them, marching toward their objective post haste. De Lattre describes their movement along the aptly named Route des Maures (Route of the Moors), "Throughout its length wound an uninterrupted column of goumiers, trotting along in single file with their mules, bare footed, their hob-nailed boots hanging about their necks or slung at their belts with their tin helmets. The endless striped djellabas gave the landscape an African appearance."

Along the way, in their typical Goumier manner, some of them began to "requisition" civilian and military cars and trucks to help them arrive at their objective sooner. These were soon abandoned, however, as the occasional sniper fire turned heavier and the tribesmen were forced to take cover.

Meanwhile at Aubagne, about eight miles from Marseilles, the appearance of the French tanks provoked a real fire fight with three battalions of well prepared German infantry supported by artillery, 75s and 105s, plus the usual array of machine guns and mortars. The French armor, unable to flank the town because the fields and roads around it were so thoroughly mined, attacked directly through the village.

The assault began on the twenty-first, but by 1000 hours Colonel Durasoy's 2nd Curassiers (tanks) and Commandant le Tang's 3rd Zouaves (the infantry that was an organic part of the armored division) had only reached the church quarter and could go no further. More infantry was needed to clear a way for the tanks.

When Colonel de Latour's 2nd GTM arrived at the Col de l'Ange it was ordered to aid the French armor by attacking Aubagne from north and south. De Latour split his command and the attack went in from both directions at 1300 hours. The fighting was fierce. Like all French towns, Aubagne was a place of stone and concrete buildings and walls, as well as thick hedges, and its narrow streets and alleyways were perfect for defense. The struggle was close up and at point blank range.

In the combat in the south part of town, the 2nd GTM's 1st Tabor had two captains, both Goum commanders, killed. In the north the inevitable savage counter attack took the Germans right into the command post of the 15th Tabor, where the clerks and signalmen repulsed their attackers with grenades. By 1800 hours the Goumiers of the 15th had entered the town, after storming a position defended by more than a dozen guns. The 1st Tabor was already in the heart of town by that time, but it was not until late the next morning that Aubagne was completely in French hands.

While the fighting at Aubagne was still going on, Guillaume split his two other Groups into separate task forces, the 1st GTM (Colonel Leblanc) swinging north to approach Marseilles from that direction while the 3rd GTM (Lieutenant-Colonel Massiet du Biest) stayed along the coastline, moving toward the port city from the south. The 1st GTM headed for the Aix-Marseilles road and soon ran into heavy opposition. At Cadoline and Peypin they were forced into lively fire fights and ended up storming those key positions. They took some 800 prisoners, sent them to the rear and marched on.

When the Goumiers reached the northern outskirts of the city they ran into a huge military complex dominated by a fortress and a series of concrete casements, well protected by artillery, machine guns, wire and mines. In addition, the surrounding houses and walled gardens had also been turned into heavily armed strong points—all with such picturesque names as *Tante Rosa* (Aunt Rose) and *Moulin de Diable* (the Devil's Mill). To enter Marseilles from the north you had to get past these fortifications—and to do that you would need tanks and heavy artillery. The attackers had none.

The Goumiers settled down to a siege. The scene was hellish. The area was an industrial suburb dotted with concrete factories and lime kilns, and the flying bullets chipped off sections of wall that mixed with limestone dust and gunpowder. A constant pall hung over the neighborhood, adding to the horror of machine gun and mortar fire. Casualties were heavy, the Goumiers losing more than one hundred men, including five officers.

The Germans were taking their licks, too. Leblanc had cut off the road from Montigues, which was virtually the last contact the Marseilles garrison had with the outside world. On the

26th he tried to take the Tante Rosa position, but the assault was beaten back. Four artillery batteries under Colonel von Hanstein, commander of the northern sector of the city, had turned the buildings into a seemingly unassailable redoubt. That same day the Germans asked for a truce to evacuate their more seriously wounded. All their doctors were dead, and they needed an ambulance. In a chivalric gesture amid the horror, Leblanc supplied one, and twenty enemy wounded were carried into the French lines. The fighting continued.

In the meanwhile, the Algerians of the 7th RTA had reached the eastern suburbs of the city. De Lattre had ordered de Monsabert to wait for reinforcements before entering Marseilles proper, for he knew that his advance forces were badly outnumbered and could be slaughtered in any heavy street fighting. Also the thousands of inhabitants of France's second largest city had not been evacuated, and the idea of civilian casualties weighed heavily on de Lattre's mind.

But de Monsabert saw it otherwise. Here was an opportunity, and when he realized that there was a civilian insurrection going on inside the city, led by the FFI (French Forces of the Interior, the *maquisards*), he felt his troops were needed here and now. He gave the word to Colonel Chappuis, commanding the Algerian regiment, and the Tirailleurs entered the city. Soon, guided by the local FFI, they were engaged in serious street fighting. Upon learning of the situation inside the city, de Lattre, as flexible as he was hot headed, approved de Monsabert's action.

While this was going on, the 2nd GTM, its work ended at Aubagne, joined the 3rd Group in moving toward the southern coast. Using their mountaineering skills, the Goumiers climbed the St. Cyr and Gradule massifs by goat path and took out more of Marseilles outer defenses with mortar and machine gun. The 2nd GTM then found itself on Route Nationale 9, headed directly for the city suburbs.

But its 6th Tabor, in action at St. Loup, was in trouble. The 11th Goum was caught by machine gun and artillery fire on the grounds of the town's ancient château. It took cover in a part of the château itself and was in a desperate situation when Commandant Méric's 1st Tabor came to the rescue. But the Germans were fighting desperately, too, and the battle lasted all day until the rest of the 6th Tabor arrived. That was too much for the Germans. The survivors surrendered.

It was a great haul for the Goums. From the huge underground caverns of the château came more than 1,200 German prisoners of war. There were fifty officers, including three colonels, plus General Boie, chief of the Marseilles *Kommandatur.* Sending their prisoners to the rear, the 2nd GTM headed straight for the city, while the 3rd GTM continued southwest along the coast.

Arriving on the outskirts of Marseilles, de Latour's men turned the Hippodrome, the racetrack in Brevy Park, into a battleground, defeated the German outposts there and plunged into the heart of town. (Apparently de Gaulle's injunction against using the Goumiers in cities was roundly ignored.) There they joined hands with the Tirailleurs in cleaning out that sector of Marseilles between Notre Dame de la Garde and the Pointe du Pharo, an old part of town where every building had been turned into a fortress and every narrow street and alleyway was a trap. It was an exhausting house to house shoot, but by midday of the twenty-seventh the enemy had been driven back to the Vieux Porte. The 6th Tabor closed in on the south side of the old Fort St. Nicholas, the last holdout, while a company of Tirailleurs kept the east face contained. Captain Crosia, Chappuis' information officer and an expert negotiator, then arranged for the evacuation of the many famished and sick women, children and old men who had taken refuge in the underground tunnels of the fort. At 1700 hours the fort surrendered and 300 Germans gave themselves up to the 11th Goum.

A short time before, de Lattre had ordered the remainder of the 3rd Algerian Division plus two sections of tanks and a section of tank destroyers to leave the mopping up of Toulon to the 9th DIC and the 1st DFL and hurry to Marseilles to help there. Now there units arrived to support another attack north of the city by the 1st GTM. When the Goumiers launched their new assault on the still resisting fortifications of Tante Rose and the Moulin de Diable, the defenders fought just as fanatically as before, but this time French armor and some newly landed artillery made the difference. The Germans were crushed, many quite literally under the tracks of the French tanks. They fought to the death, refusing to surrender, obeying Hitler's order, "Defend Marseilles to the last cartridge!"

Hanstein asked for another cease fire to evacuate his wounded. Leblanc replied, "It is impossible for me to evacuate your wounded every evening, for their numbers will continue to grow while my medical resources for them do not increase. This, therefore, is the last time I will respond to your appeal. Tomorrow our heavy and siege artillery, made available by our victory at Toulon, will reduce you to such a state that it will be useless to think of transporting the wounded."[10]

Hanstein understood that it was all over, but his superiors did not. At this time there were two separate battles going on in the heart of the city, one for the area of Notre Dame de la Garde, the great Marseilles cathedral, and the other for the six kilometers of port facilities—and the Germans were losing them both. They still had men and ammunition, but the French now occupied almost all of Marseilles. And as more of their troops were landing, the attackers were growing stronger while the Germans, cut off from all outside help, were rapidly growing weaker. It was, indeed, all over.

All that remained for the French now was the mopping up to the south of the city, and the Goumiers of the 3rd GTM were busily engaged in that. They had marched along the southern coast overcoming a series of batteries and strongholds from Prado Beach to Cap Croisette. When they had needed heavy artillery support they got it from the Allied ships lying off the shoreline, and it was naval gunfire that tipped the scale in the fall of Vielle Chapelle, the Pointe Rouge and Château de Mondron. When the Goumiers of the 3rd GTM finally reached Marseilles they had 1,500 prisoners in hand—and the southern shores of France had been swept clean of enemy troops.

Now everything came together. On August 28 General Hans Schaeffer, the commanding officer of the 244th Infantry Division and the defender of Marseilles, officially surrendered the city to de Monsabert. On that same day Toulon capitulated. France's great naval base and Marseilles, its largest commercial port, were now in Allied hands. Although the docks had been thoroughly demolished by the defeated Germans they would soon be back in operation again, liberated by a proud new French army. The conquest of the city had been accomplished weeks ahead of schedule, and once again the tribesmen from the Atlas had shared in the glory.

After a waterfront victory parade, de Lattre put the Goumiers in reserve. Now he was ordered to provide a force to guard the eastern border with Italy, high in the Alps. What better troops for that purpose than the Moroccan Goumiers?

Leblanc's 1st GTM was selected for the job. In view of the continuing shortages, transport to the Alpine regions was not without difficulty, but eventually enough trucks were rounded up to convey the Goumiers to their destination. Alas, they had to leave their precious mules in Marseilles.

Since the landings the Alpine border passes had been guarded by the paratroopers of the 1st Allied Airborne Task Force, and those troops would continue to screen the area from the Mediterranean to the Col de Larche (Larche Pass), some sixty miles from the sea. But the region north of that, deep in the lofty Alpine massif, would be taken over by the Goumiers, fresh from their triumph in Marseilles, plus elements of the newly arriving 2nd Moroccan Division.

The first task the Goumiers had to accomplish in their new home among those forbidding peaks was to replace the mules they left behind. This was easier than expected, for the local villagers, delighted to see French forces in command once more, were most cooperative. If one town could not meet all the immediate needs for animals, the mayor would telephone the next village, which would gladly supply more. In very short order enough of their favorite mode of transport were found to keep the Goumiers happy and ready for the next order of business—the thorough reconnaissance for which they had become famous.

While they had received some information from the paratroopers they were relieving, the French officers were not satisfied. Patrols were sent out, and what they found was not encouraging. There were many, many more of the enemy than they had expected—and they had artillery. The Germans had established outposts in the high mountains and occupied some of the border towns and were determined not to be thrown out.

The patrols were costly. Many Goumiers were casualties in their unavoidable contacts with the enemy; for instance, a scouting party from Lieutenant-Colonel Colbert's Tabor came back from a reconnaissance of Mont Genevre with ten wounded and five dead, including an adjudant.

With considerable difficulty in the appalling terrain, the French had brought up artillery and soon heavy artillery duels shook the mountain passes. Then the Goums and Tirailleurs attacked in force. They cleaned out Briançon and Mondane, driving the enemy back through the passes.

The Alpine terrain in that area was particularly difficult, even for the Goumiers. They found the footing around the Col de Larche and the Plateau des Bouchieres extremely unstable. It was all shale, a rock made of densely packed clay that split easily into layers, of a type unique to the territory and strange to the Moroccans. They had never before experienced this kind of stone that sheared off underfoot as they marched, making the uphill going doubly difficult and the downhill even more dangerous. Nor had they previously suffered such murderous effects as when the brittle shale was struck by enemy bullets and shellfire, with the flying shards more deadly than the shrapnel itself. Jacques Augarde, a lieutenant in the 1st GTM, tells the harrowing story of his Goumiers trying to reach the body of a young French *aspirant* (cadet) lying in the open under enemy fire, and then when it was recovered with the bullets whizzing around, of their trials as the Goumiers carried their precious burden down the Alpine mountainside, slipping and sliding on the treacherous footing.[11]

The Alpine fighting lasted through September and resulted in the inevitable heavy casualties, including the death of Lieutenant-Colonel Colbert and many of his Goumiers. At that time the enemy made no more serious attempts to attack through the Alps, and the Moroccans were eventually replaced by units of the FFI. The Tabors were happy to leave that area and rejoin the main body of the army, and once again they had proven their ability to adjust to any situation in any terrain.

August and September had been hard days for every fighting man in southern France, but particularly for the Germans. They had been surprised by the suddenness of the landings and devastated by the loss of Marseilles and Toulon. Now they were ordered by Berlin to evacuate the entire southern region of France, which they immediately started to do. They took terrible losses on the way. By September the Nineteenth Army was hardly an army any more. Its divisions were cut to pieces, its regiments filled in with odd units of police, Luftwaffe and service troops and ineffective "Ost" battalions from Russia like the 360th Cossack horse cavalry. And there were thousands of deserters, stragglers and POWs. But the army struggled on, decimated but never quite destroyed by its American and French pursuers.

The Allies, too, were having their troubles. Patch's Seventh Army had only one corps, General Truscott's with only three divisions, while many of de Lattre's troops were still landing on the beaches. Besides a manpower shortage there was also a lack of ammunition, gasoline and transport. Although Marseilles had been captured, the port facilities wouldn't be ready for use for weeks.

But Allied morale was high, and although the troops were tired, the pursuit continued. Important cities and towns were wrested from the Germans, including Lyon, Grenoble and others. And while the troops were fighting, the Allied staffs were planning future moves and reorganizing to meet the armies' present needs. As more troops landed and reached de Lattre he split his Army B into two corps, I Corps under Lieutenant-General Emile Béthouart and II Corps commanded by the tough, reliable *Africain,* de Monsabert, whom he called "that devil of a man." De Lattre's command was now, if not yet officially at least provisionally, the First French Army. It was indeed the first complete, independent army the French could muster since rejoining the Allies in 1942, and its existence was a great boost to French morale. And the tribesmen from the Atlas were an important part of it.

Now that de Monsabert was promoted to corps commander, the leadership of that most effective and experienced fighting body, the 3rd Algerian Infantry Division, was up for grabs. De Lattre didn't hesitate. On September 1, 1944, he named Augustin Guillaume to that prestigious post. It was both a joy and a sorrow for Guillaume. He was proud to take command of such a distinguished division, but sad to leave his beloved Goumiers. One compensation was that the 3rd DIA also had its origins in Africa, and another was that the Tabors would continue to work closely with the Algerians, as they had in the past.

Then, too, the Goumiers would be left in good hands. Colonel Hogard, the new Commandant of Goums, was a tough, resolute and experienced officer, and Leblanc, de Latour and Massiet du Biest still commanded their tribesmen.

The Goums, relieved of their duties in the Alpine regions, were now given a new assignment—an attack on the German defenses in the Vosges Mountains. The Germans had slowed their retreat, their resistance had stiffened and they had formed a line to block off the Vosges and the Belfort Gap, the latter being that area below the Vosges and north of the Jura Mountains that had long been a traditional invasion route to Germany.

On September 15 de Lattre's forces *officially* became the First French Army and was no longer under command of Patch's Seventh Army. Now both armies were combined to form the Sixth Army Group under General Jacob Devers. This hardly changed the tactical plans at all. The high command had determined that the First French Army was to fight its way through the Belfort Gap while the Seventh U.S. Army was to engage the enemy in the Vosges. But before the Belfort operation de Monsabert's II Corps was to support the Americans in the southern section of the mountains. And that's where the Goums came in.

The Vosges Mountains encompassed an area about seventy miles long from north to south and some thirty to forty miles wide. Unlike the generally open Atlas where the Goumiers had lived, and the rocky Italian ranges where they had so successfully fought, the Vosges were, in part, heavily forested, dark and dank. Its terrain was perfect for defense, and the Germans had made the most of it. Not only had the Todt organization been put to work on its extensive field fortifications, but large numbers of French civilians had been drafted for construction work as well. And these defensive works displayed all the German genius for the devilish application of mines, booby traps, machine-gun nests, mortars and artillery. Even the weather seemed to conspire against the attackers. The mountains were wet. There was almost constant rain at this time of year, with its accompanying fog and mud, and swift running streams and rivers criss-crossed the wooded hills. A pall of gloom seemed constantly to hang over the region, even where the occasional tiny villages, rolling fields and valley farmlands split the mountainsides.

The Americans of the Seventh Army on the French flank were holding a strategic ridgeline called Longegoutte, but were now ordered to move north. The movement was supposed to take place on the nights of October 4 and 5, with French troops occupying the American positions under cover of darkness. This was agreed to by de Lattre as he wanted to use that terrain as a start line for his planned attack through the Vosges to the plains of Alsace. But when the first French troops arrived, they were greeted with rifle and machine gun fire. The Germans were already occupying the American positions—the GIs had pulled out on the second and third by mistake! Now the French would have to fight for the ridge.

In organizing the Vosges attack de Lattre once again combined the Goums and the Tirailleurs, the 2nd and 3rd GTM with the 3rd DIA, plus a battalion of Gardes Mobiles that had just reached the scene—all under that hard-bitten *Africain*, General Guillaume. In early October this determined "Guillaume Group" started their assault up the hills of the Longegoutte Forest, a thick, fog-shrouded woodland infested with Germans.

Right from the start the going was tough. The Germans, well dug in with covered fortifications to protect them from tree bursts, fought with the usual Teutonic energy and skill, and the casualties among the French were heavy. The struggle was generally northward, up the southern slopes of Longegoutte. The French had nearly reached its crest when the German 338th Division counterattacked all along the entire front. The fighting was horrendous, later described by de Lattre in his colorful manner as "at once fierce, breathless and merciless." Much of the time it was hand to hand, and no quarter asked or given. The Goumiers actually welcomed the counter-attack since it brought the enemy out of their casements and pill-boxes and into the open. But the Germans gave as good as they got and for a while it looked like the power of their assault would drive the French forces back down the mountainside.

Guillaume had divided his force into two units, Tactical Group 1 under General Duval of the Algerian Division, combining the 2nd GTM and the 3rd RTA, and Tactical Group 2 commanded by Colonel Chappuis and consisting of the 3rd GTM and the 7th RTA. When the German counter-attack struck, Chappuis' TG 2 on the western section of the line held its ground, but the enemy broke through on the right between the Col de Moribeux (Moribeux Pass) and the Col de Rahme, isolating some forward French units. There followed some thirty-six more hours of confused fighting much of it hand to hand, with death and injury on all sides. At the end the Germans fell back and the French found themselves at the crest of Longegoutte, hardly any better off than they were at the start of the fray.

Now they were overlooking the winding Moselotte River. Once again the Goumiers attacked and forced their way across the strongly defended stream at a point between Theofosse and Saulxures. The miserable weather became worse, with the rain turning into unusually early snow and biting cold, yet Guillaume kept attacking the mountain crests north of the Moselotte. There was ferocious resistance, but the French ended up in possession of the heights of Piquante Pierre (Prickly Pete), Rondfaing, Tete des Cerfs (Stag's Head) and the high ground on the west side of Cornimont.

But the troops were exhausted; many of the Goumiers had been fighting with little pause since Tunisia. And there was sickness, too, particularly colds, flu, pneumonia, trenchfoot and injuries caused by frostbite, all as a result of the severe

Goumiers wade ashore on Elba.

weather. De Lattre decided it was time for a rest, and he ordered a brief pause in the attack.

It was brief indeed. On October 16 the Goumiers attacked again, this time ending on top of the Haut du Faing, but heavy French losses without the possibility of replacements brought any further attacks to a halt. De Lattre decided that a breakthrough in the Vosges before the outbreak of winter was impossible. He ordered a temporary halt in that sector, and continued with his planning for the attack through the Belfort Gap.

But there was to be one more French effort in the mountains. The Americans of the Seventh Army (using Leclerc's attached French 2nd Armored Division) were planning an assault on Strasbourg to the north, and they needed a diversionary action in the south. De Lattre obliged, and the Guillaume Group went on the attack once again. This time the target area was the Rochesson sector, and the assault was made with considerable artillery and, weather permitting, air support. The opposition by troops of the skeletonized 198th and 278th Divisions was fierce, but after forty-eight hours of fighting, the French held all the crests, and two German counterattacks failed to dislodge them. The diversionary mission of Guillaume's Goumiers and Tirailleurs accomplished, de Monsabert called off the attacks. The attempt of the French II Corps to crash through the southern Vosges to the plains of Alsace and the Rhine was over for the time being, but holding and patrol actions continued.

While the October Vosges campaign might be called less than successful in its outcome, actually it accomplished a great deal. The French not only gained a stronger foothold in the mountains, but dozens of villages and hamlets were liberated, free at last from the often harsh German occupation. Wiese's already crippled Nineteenth Army was further decimated—the French claimed 3,300 Germans killed and more than 2,000 captured from the first to the eighteenth of October, with French losses at 450 killed and 2,000 wounded during the same period. Furthermore, the enemy had to weaken other sectors of their front to supply reinforcements for their troops in the mountains, and were even forced to bring fresh troops from Germany to meet the threat. The French drive through the Vosges, in spite of the terrible sacrifices of the Goumiers and Tirailleurs, was certainly a worthwhile effort.

Although the main effort to clear a way to the plains of Alsace through the Vosges was essentially over, de Lattre did not want his Belfort intentions to be known to the enemy. An elaborate deception plan was put in effect to take the Germans' attention away from the Belfort regions, and lead them to believe that the principal attack would still be in the high Vosges. This trickery included increased radio communications throughout the mountain area, plus the establishment of fake headquarters and bogus troop movements, all picked up by enemy spies and radio detection devices and reported back to German headquarters. But the most important part of the deception was to keep up the pressure in the Vosges, and this was up to Guillaime's 3rd DIA—and, of course, the Goums.

So the attacks in the mountains resumed. In early November the French stormed the Col d'Oderen, 3,000-feet high, an assault deeply involving the 3rd GTM. Here the French met heavy opposition, including the 169th Infantry Division, completely refitted after battling in Finland, plus as many as fifteen other infantry battalions. The fighting was intense, *oahad oahad* as the Goumiers said—one on one, hand to hand—but they took the important peaks in spite of violent enemy reaction.

Lieutenant-Colonel Leblanc's 1st GTM was also fighting hard in the Col de Bussang region with the 12th Tabor conquering the Breton Matten, the Belacker Wald and the Mittel Rainskopf, while the 3rd Tabor cleaned out Hill 800 and the Hoher Kopf. The Goumiers also took the Stufthopf, but were thrown off by a counterattack. They then took another route, and by the end of the day had recaptured their original objective.

Then Leblanc's men descended from their newly captured heights and entered Rimbach. They were now in a position overlooking the important town of St. Amarin and, at last, were actually in Alsace! The officers were happy to reach their long sought objective, the Goumiers caught the spirit, and the entire 1st GTM carried on in a holiday mood. The fighting continued. The Goums entered Mitzach where they surprised the Germans and put them to flight.[12]

But the entrance of French forces into Alsace had stiffened enemy resistance and the 3rd GTM, still in the mountains, were having a hard time. Enemy troops had infiltrated their positions on the wooded summit of the Ventron in a counter attack that had the German soldiers dodging from tree to tree lobbing grenades at the defending Goumiers. The fighting lasted all afternoon with the Germans finally defeated, leaving twenty bodies on the mountain slopes.

By early December du Biest's Goumiers were across the Col de Brabant, but the thrill of being in Alsace had begun to wear off as they continued fighting along the "rute of the crests" toward their objectives on the plains below.

De Lattre's mind was now fully on the Belfort Gap. The terrain there was much kinder to the attackers than that of the mountains, but although the fighting would be fierce the French would be able to use their armor with greater effect. And many of the troops of Béthouart's I Corps who were to do much of the Belfort fighting were in reserve while the Goums were engaged in their recent struggles along the ridgelines. They would be well rested for the new challenge. All in all, it appeared that the chances for success were excellent.

The attack started on November 14, right after a heavy snowfall, and the Germans were taken by surprise. Because of the continued aggressive patrolling of the Goumiers in the mountains to the north, they thought that the main French effort would be there. They were unprepared when Béthouart's infantry and armor struck.

The fighting lasted all through November as town after town fell to the French. One column of the 1st Armored Division made a virtually unopposed dash eastward and actually arrived at the Rhine at Rosenau, the first of any Allied troops to reach the river in the offensives of World War II. Unfortunately, grand strategy demanded that all the Allied armies throughout Europe should be lined up on the west bank before a crossing could be attempted, and the French had to hold where they were.[13] However, an artillery battery was brought up to fire across the river—the first French shells to land on German soil since the spring of 1940. The gesture was more ceremonial than practical, but it certainly made the French feel good. "What a moment to be alive! What humiliations avenged!" wrote de Lattre.

On the twenty-fifth the city of Belfort and its surrounding fortifications fell just a short time after Mulhouse, the second most important city in Alsace, was liberated, bringing the Belfort Gap drive virtually to an end. The Goums were not inactive in these operations, for their continued presence with the 3rd DIA in the southern Vosges kept the Germans busy. And they would soon have more work to do, for Alsace was not yet completely free.

While de Lattre's troops were mopping up in the Belfort Gap and Patch's Seventh Army had reached Strasbourg to the north, there was a large salient west of the Rhine that the Germans were determined to keep, even though their Nineteenth Army was falling apart. This was known as the Colmar Pocket. It was a bulge of irregular shape, extending from its forty-mile base along the river to some thirty miles westward at its deepest part. Its circumference was not a solid defensive line, but a series of strong points—fortified towns, crossroads and bridges with the usual fiendish array of mines, booby traps and wire covered by riflemen, machine guns, mortars, tanks and artillery. It was surrounded by the First French Army, with de Monsabert's II Corps spread along the northern rim and Béthouart's I Corps to the south.

To the Fuehrer, holding the Colmar Pocket was a matter of historical prestige. In modern times, the French territory Alsace had been conquered by the Germans in the Franco-Prussian War of 1870, retaken by the French in World War I and occupied by the Germans again in 1940. Although the majority of the population regarded themselves as French, the Germans would have none of it, and the idea of it being back in French hands was anathema to Hitler. The enthusiastic welcome the population gave to their French liberators, even to the exotic and scary looking Berbers of the Tabors,[14] was salt in German wounds.

Although the German leader was at this time in early December preparing for his surprise attack in the Ardennes, his attention was still drawn to this last occupied portion of southern Alsace. To this end he created a new command, Army Group Oberrheim, and appointed his terrifying police chief, Heinrich Himmler, to be its head. To emphasize its importance, Himmler was to report directly to the Fuehrer himself—and hold the Colmar Pocket.

It was a strange set-up. Himmler, not by any stretch of the imagination a soldier, in turn named Lieutenant-General Siegfried Rasp to replace General Wiese as commander of the Nineteenth Army, and then turned his own attention to obtaining everything he could in the way of supplies, equipment and personnel for the newly rejuvenated command. As a consummate politician, Himmler was very good at this. He knew the right people in the Reich, and if there was anything to be had, he got it. The result was a newly strengthened Nineteenth Army with nine more infantry divisions and two new tank brigades, although all were under strength and of varying quality.[15] The new offensive was code-named "Nordwind."

At the same time, the First French Army, which had been given the job of eliminating the salient, was also strengthened by the addition of the U.S. 36th Division (later replaced by the U.S. 3rd Division) and General Leclerc's famous 2nd French Armored Division, so it seemed to the high command that its task of cleaning out the Colmar Pocket would not be too difficult. But there were problems. De Lattre's men were exhausted, their equipment worn out, and there were few replacements for those who had been lost in battle. The best foot soldiers, the Goumiers and Tirailleurs, were done in for they had done much of the fighting and taken the heaviest losses. For the most part the FFI volunteers, whom de Lattre was using to fill in the weak spots, were not working out as well as he had hoped. Try as they might, they had neither the training nor experience of the tough professionals from North Africa who were taking the brunt of the fighting.

De Lattre was of the opinion that the metropolitan French were letting the army down by not volunteering for military service in large enough numbers, and he let his political superiors in Paris know of his feelings in no uncertain terms. There were other political issues, too. Ledere, whose 2nd Armored Division was newly transferred from Patch's Seventh Army, didn't really want to serve under de Lattre or de Monsabert. He had been part of de Gaulle's Free French movement from its very beginnings, and had trekked with his original tiny command across the Sahara from central Africa, fighting all the way. His group had eventually joined the British Eighth Army battling Rommel in the Libyan desert while his current superiors were still serving, albeit reluctantly, under the Vichy regime.

But in spite of there difficulties, de Lattre had his orders to clean out the Colmar Pocket. In early December he decided it was time. He gave the order, and while Béthouart's I Corps in the south was held up by supply difficulties including a serious Jack of artillery ammunition, II Corps in the northwest corner of the pocket crashed ahead. Using the 3rd DIA and all three groups of Goumiers, de Monsabert attacked through the mountains on a line linking the Col du Bonhomme on the right and the city of Selestat in the plains on the left.

The first object of the assault was the village of Orbey, on a direct line with the city of Colmar itself. As the attack started, the weather closed in. Rain, sleet and heavy snow stopped all air activity, blinded artillery observation and even slowed the infantry for three days. Then the attack resumed.

Orbey was in the center of a vast basin rimmed by German-held heights. On the right the attackers were the Tirailleurs of the 1st RTA, supported in the Kayserberg Forest by the Goumiers of de Latour's 2nd GTM, while on the left the assault forces included Leblanc's 1st GTM and the armor of the 2nd and 3rd Spahis. The Goums of the 2nd Group stormed the village of Lapoutrie and captured the heights overlooking Orbey, allowing Colonel Guillebaud's 4th Tunisian Tirailleurs and a mixed squadron of Sherman tanks and M-10 tank destroyers to enter Orbey itself. In this operation the French captured more than 5,000 prisoners, but the attackers were exhausted and there were no replacements for the fallen. On December 24 de Lattre ordered the attacks to cease and the troops to hold where they were.

Then, at the beginning of January, the greatly reinforced German Nineteenth Army went on the offensive, with the main German effort directed at splitting Patch's Seventh Army in two. In order to prevent this, the Allied high command gave the order to withdraw the exposed units that were in the path of the enemy drive. This would entail the abandonment of Strasbourg, the chief city of Alsace, which had been liberated by the Allies just a short time before. De Gaulle—and de Lattre—objected strenuously.

There followed a heated debate at the highest level, with the French pointing out the political importance of the city and what would happen to its inhabitants if the Germans were allowed to reoccupy this proud symbol of French sovereignty. Eisenhower finally relented and the withdrawal was halted short of Strasbourg. Its defense was turned over to the First French Army, and de Lattre immediately pulled the 3rd DIA—and most of the Goums—out of their Colmar Pocket positions and sent them north to defend the Strasbourg area. A defensive line was created from Krafft, just south of Strasbourg, that extended southwest to Selestat, where it was manned by the 6th Tabor of the 2nd GTM, while other French elements fanned out to the north.

On January 15, in spite of the German offensive, de Lattre gave the order for the First French Army to resume the drive on the Colmar Pocket. Furious infantry and tank battles followed, hand to hand combat and artillery duels, all in the terrible weather of the worst winter Europe had seen in many years. There was as much as three feet of snow—and then there was a sudden thaw, and mud and overflowing streams and rivers. Still the fighting went on, with the French, now reinforced by more American troops, gradually capturing the fortified towns, one by one, and the Germans falling back toward the Rhine. Finally, on February 9 the last of the Colmar Pocket was cleared and the battered Germans withdrew across the river. [16]

While the Goumiers had played little part in the last acts of the Colmar story—elements of the 3rd GTM had joined the 9th Zouaves in the capture of the village of Munster[17]—most of the Tabors had been active elsewhere, fighting the Germans fiercely for the possession of the area below Strasbourg. As Colmar fell the Germans had also retreated north across the Moder, and a strange quiet descended on the front.

The French troops used this welcome pause to repair and reorganize. The infantry cleaned their rifles and machine guns, the armored units worked on their tanks and armored cars. Replacements were at last brought in to fill some of the depleted ranks and all hands continued their training. A plan to rebuild the ranks of the Tirailleurs, long in the making, was put in effect. The men of the third regiment of the 3rd DIA, were used as replacements for the other two regiments, and an entirely new group of locally raised Frenchmen replaced the original African regiment. The Tirailleurs were up to strength again as the newcomers and the old hands used these few weeks of quiet to train together.

The Goumiers needed this time as much as the others. They set their tin hats aside for the moment and rewound their turbans. They cleaned their rifles and sharpened their knives. And, like the other troops, they trained. There was little change in personnel; by and large the officers of the Tabors stayed the same and the Goumiers were still the Berbers of the Atlas.

De Lattre and his staff were as busy as ever, planning the next move. All along the Allied front the troops were readying for the last phase of the war, the plunge across the Rhine into Germany. The commander had received his orders for the mission of the First French Army in this final push—and he didn't like them. According to these orders he was supposed to move into the enemy's country in what he considered a subordinate role, guarding the rear of Patch's Seventh Army and not exactly tearing at the vitals of the enemy. This was certainly not a role to suit the aggressive de Lattre. He at once complained to de Gaulle and de Gaulle went to Eisenhower. There were more high level discussions. In the end de Lattre more or less got his way. He feigned satisfaction, but in his subtle manner made unofficial changes, coordinating his plans with the local American forces without reporting all of his intentions to his own superiors.

In the end the plan was to attack along the Moder River where the withdrawal of the American Seventh Army had stopped short of Strasbourg. On the German side this was the so-called "Annemarie Line," a string of fortified positions along the southern edge of the Haguenau Forest that stretched from Bischwiller near the Rhine westward to the eastern slopes of the Low Vosges. Drawn up west of the Haguenau Forest were two American divisions, the veteran 36th Infantry and the raw 14th Armored. On the east side of the forest were the French troops de Lattre had designated as Task Force Monsabert—the always reliable 3rd DIA, CC6 of the Fifth Armored Division and the Goumiers of the 1st and 2nd GTM. For the purposes of the coming operation TF Monsabert was attached to General Brooks' American VI Corps.

When the Goumiers of the 1st GTM infiltrated into the green hell of the Haguenau, they were spread out about six miles further west than they were supposed to be. This was no accident. It was a maneuver carefully planned by de Lattre, always thinking ahead, to put the First French Army in an advantageous position for future operations. The movement west into the American zone was done without the knowledge of higher headquarters, but with the willing cooperation of the American troops on the ground, who were quite happy to shorten their lines. It was an excellent example of Allied agreement on the front line level, without interference by a higher command. A command, incidentally, that concurred after the fact.

However, all this made little difference to the Goumiers. They had the immediate problem of advancing through the wilderness and flushing out the Germans who were doggedly opposing them with rifle, machine gun and grenade. And there were countless mines, plus the usual collection of ingenious booby traps. Although the Goumiers were becoming quite adept at disarming them, these devilish instruments of death took their inevitable toll.

Throughout the night of March 16 the Goumiers fought their way through the forest, breaking out on the seventeenth to take the town of Rittershoffen. They were soon on the banks of the Lauter River that marked the borderline between France and Germany. Only then did they realize they were about to cross over onto the soil of the enemy.

To the Goumiers this was heady stuff. Victory was in the air, and what de Lattre called a "fever of enthusiasm" gripped the troops. Back in Italy Guillaume had remarked to Juin that his Berbers reacted unusually well to success, and that seemed to be the case now. The Goumiers were really charged up, anxious to get across the river into Germany, even though they knew the fighting would be harder there than ever before. For on the other side they would meet the deadly obstacles of the Siegfried Line, the "impenetrable" belt of permanent fortifications that guarded Germany from a vengeful outside world.

Indeed, in this particular sector, the "Westwall" obstacles were especially deadly. First of all, they were set in a forest area, the Bienwald, and the Germany had made full use of the thickly wooded terrain for maximum protection and concealment. The main line was a series of concrete bunkers sunk into the ground so as to be almost invisible, and laid out in staggered rows to take every advantage of the killing possibilities of interlocking fire. Even worse, these were surrounded by a network of barbed wire, interspersed with steel abatis and festooned with thousands of mines and booby traps cleverly arranged to stop even the most aggressive infantry and tank teams. Before entering this garden of death the French had brought up every piece of artillery available and thoroughly covered the area with shellfire. Then the infantry went in.

Leblanc's Goumiers crossed the Lauter at Sheibenhard where a bridgehead had been established by elements of the 3rd DIA, and on March 21 they reached the first obstacles of the Siegfried Line. At that point a wall of small arms fire greeted them, and all forward movement stopped as the tribesmen were forced to hit the ground. Then they found they could *crawl* forward, their earth colored *djellabas* making them nearly invisible as they moved on hands and knees through the underbrush. Booby traps took a heavy toll, but they managed to dig out some of the antitank mines by hand (they had no mine detectors), cut through the wire and return the small arms fire as best they could. They proceeded this way, actually crawling for several miles, until utter exhaustion brought them to a halt. Casualties were heavy. Commandant Absecat was killed, as were fifty-five men in the 101st Goum alone, sixteen by mines and booby traps. But, miraculously, the Goumiers had made a path for the tanks, and that turned the tide.

The fighting lasted all night, the French infantry and the American tanks gradually winkling the enemy out of their fortifications. After recovering their breaths the Goumiers were at it again, the wild night lit by flashes of fire, the air filled with the pungent odor of powder and the Berber cries of "Zidou l'goudem!" By morning those Germans who were not dead or prisoner were fleeing eastward toward the Rhine and trying desperately to cross to relative—and temporary—safety.

For the Goumiers of the 1st GTM it turned into a manhunt, with the tribesmen pursuing their quarry all the way to Hagenbush near the Rhine. Here they were met by their brothers of the 2nd GTM who, along with the Tirailleurs of the 4th RTT, had just taken Neuburg. Together the North Africans, Moroccan Goumier and Tunisian Tirailleur, rounded up a huge number of prisoners and chased the surviving enemy across the river. By March 24 the French had broken through the Siegfried Line everywhere. Next stop—the Rhine.

CHAPTER 5

Across the Rhine—
The Last Laugh

"My dear general, you must cross the Rhine, even if the Americans do not help you and you are obliged to use boats. The matter is one of the highest national interest. Karlsruhe and Stuttgart expect you, even if they don't want you."[1]

That was the message de Lattre received from de Gaulle on March 29, 1945. He passed it along to II Corps and told de Monsabert to get started across the Rhine. "Impossible!" replied de Monsabert. "Yes, I know," said his chief. "But do it anyway."

Here was the problem. II Corps now occupied the west bank of the Rhine from Lauterbach to Speyer. I Corps occupied it further south, but crossings there were impractical because on the opposite bank was the mountainous, wooded terrain of the Black Forest, more heavily fortified and gunned than the regions further north. The French had the permission of higher headquarters to cross as far north as Speyer, which would put them well north of the Black Forest and enable them to come southeast toward Stuttgart, avoiding the heavily defended forest area. For Stuttgart, the capital of Württemburg province, was the great prize.

Patch's Seventh Army had already crossed the river north of Speyer and was fighting its way south with official orders to capture the coveted city. It was de Lattre's intention, spurred on by de Gaulle, to cross the Rhine and beat Patch to Stuttgart. The problems for the French were enormous. Their forces were scattered, and worse, they had little means of crossing, having only a comparatively few small boats. These included fifty-five M-2 motor boats, each with a capacity of twelve, and fifteen "Stormboats," six-man assault craft with outboard motors. There were also a dozen rubber boats available—complete with paddles!

However, the First French Army had an ace in the hole. It was the disassembled sections of a ten-ton timber bridge that had been hidden from the Germans during the occupation of Alsace. Colonel Dromard, the First Army chief engineer, had recovered these invaluable parts months before and had local factories manufacture the missing components. Now he had a complete bridge ready to put in place. Somehow or other de Monsabert had also begged, borrowed and perhaps stolen additional bridging and boats from the generous General Brooks and his American VI Corps, and by a miracle of improvisation had on the night of March 30 and 31 launched the advance components of II Corps across the Rhine. The heavy equipment actually crossed on a VI Corps Bridge thanks to General Brooks.

It was not easy. The landings were opposed by the 47th Volks-grenadier Division at Speyer and the 16th VGD and elements of the SS Gebirge (Mountain) Division further south at Germersheim and Leimersheim. Artillery and small arms fire raked the boats and the bridges. Casualties were heavy, but the troops of the First French Army eventually reached the far banks, and by April 7 had taken Karlsruhe, invested Pforzheim, and had exceeded orders by penetrating further into Germany than they were supposed to. Devers, de Lattre's immediate commander, warned him to slow down; de Gaulle urged him on.

Past Karlsruhe in the Pforzheim area, wherever the terrain permitted, the French armor streaked ahead. But eventually the tanks ran into almost impassable territory, two forested massifs, the Heucheberg and the Stromberg. The tankers called for infantry. Leblanc's 1st GTM, which had crossed the Rhine at Speyer, responded.

Along with the 3rd RSAR, which operated on the meagre road net, plus the 3rd RTA, the Goumiers attacked. The Germans were well dug in and they were fighting with the do-or-die spirit of desperate men. They had been preparing their defenses for a long time and prisoners later revealed that they had expected to hold out for many months. But the North Africans were on a high, and the mountain territory was in their hands in four days. Two thousand two hundred prisoners were taken.[2]

De Lattre now had columns marching south and east throughout the provinces of Württemburg and Baden, and the French were in action everywhere. At the famous health spa of Baden-Baden a French tank stuck the barrel of its gun through a window of the once-popular casino and pulverized the machine-gun nest inside. In that same area two Goums of the 6th Tabor (2nd GTM) left Gernsbach to force the Lichtenthal Pass, defended by a German battalion with ten well dug-in artillery pieces. The pass was taken in short order. The 4th GTM, under Lieutenant-Colonel Parlange, which had just arrived from North Africa to replace the 3rd GTM, lost no time in seizing the town of Wildbad on the Gros Eng. Then an encircling movement enabled the Goumiers of the 1st GTM to meet with the Tirailleurs of the 4th RTT in surrounding two regiments of the 716th VGD and destroying them in a fierce fire fight. The survivors surrendered. Elements of de Latour's 2nd GTM had entered Freudenstadt, north of the Black Forest, and were engaged in a hot contest with its Waffen SS defenders. The Goumiers won.

On the 19th Augustin-Léon Guillaume was wounded, struck in the head and arm by shell fragments. It happened as he was riding in a jeep near Hirsau while bringing orders to the 1st and 4th GTMs. There was a lot of blood, but it hardly slowed the intrepid general—he continued in command of his hard fighting division and its attached Goums without significant pause.

As can be seen, the fighting in these last weeks of the war was wild, disconnected and confused, but de Lattre managed to keep all the threads together. In many cases the Germans resisted with as much ferocity as ever, and the Goums were hard put to overcome their well constructed defenses and artfully placed booby traps and wire. At other times, surrounded units gave up without a fight. The German civilians were, understandably, totally cowed, and the white bedsheets of surrender were displayed everywhere. They were particularly fearful of the Goumiers, whose hooded *djellabas* and scraggly beards made them seem like some avenging medieval monks.[3]

The destruction of the 716th VGD (its third regiment had surrendered en masse after the bloody defeat of the rest of the division) opened the way to Stuttgart. The French had ripped apart the German Nineteenth Army, splitting the defenders of Stuttgart from the SS corps in the Black Forest and making a path for Béthouart's I Corps to cross the Rhine and completely surround the forest area.

De Lattre was now ready to execute his orders to invest Stuttgart from the west and let the U.S. Seventh Army attack and occupy it from the north. But since the Americans were now held up by German resistance further north, why wait for them? Why not have his French troops capture this once great metropolis? Without informing his superiors of his intentions, de Lattre, whose aggressive nature never let him miss an opportunity, gave the order.

This was not the first time that de Lattre had ignored instructions from above, and General Devers, his superior, was more than a little annoyed. The Sixth Army Group Commander had planned for the 3rd U.S. Infantry Division plus the 10th Armored to sweep up the valley of the Neckar and cross the Danube to the Austrian border. He was afraid that a premature French attack on Stuttgart might cause the German

Nineteenth Army to pull out before the Seventh Army's VI Corps could bypass Stuttgart and block the major highways south of the city.[4]

There was another reason for Devers' concern. A secret intelligence mission was to accompany the Sixth Army Group to Hechingen, fifty miles south of Stuttgart, where German nuclear scientists were supposed to be working. The idea was to get there before the French did, interrogate the scientists and latch on to their documents. It was a matter of some importance, and Devers was afraid that the French action might interfere with the mission.

Certainly, since it crossed the Rhine the progress of the First French Army had been astounding. Karlsruhe had fallen on April 4, Pforzheim on the eighth. French armor had raced south along the east bank of the Rhine to a point opposite Strasbourg, covering the crossing of Béthouart's I Corps, which then struck out to the east to split the Black Forest in half. Other French troops driving down the eastern fringe of the forest area linked up with I Corps to cut off the entire northern half of the forest. Then the French forces spread out toward the south to surround the lower half, and the German troops trapped there surrendered.

The French commander's plan was to envelop Stuttgart, sending the 3rd DIA and the Goums circling around to the east to cut off any attempts by the German defenders to flee in that direction, while his armor moved directly into the city. The attacking columns started out on April 18 by crossing the inter-army boundary into the Seventh Army zone. They seized the road center of Tuebingen on the Neckar, due south of Stuttgart, trapping most of General der Artillerie Max Grimmeiss' LXIV Corps. It looked like the German LXII Corps, in a defensive position north of the city, might also be trapped if Stuttgart were surrounded. As the Germans realized their disastrous position, defenses stiffened, and on the nineteenth and twentieth, the French attack was slowed.

General Devers now saw that the French were about to take the coveted city. De Lattre's disregard of previous planning and, indeed, of specific orders, was now a *fait accompli*, so Devers made the best of a bad situation; he changed the inter-army boundary, legitimizing de Lattre's insubordinate moves.

Other French columns pushed down along the Neckar from the north by way of Esslingen, and on the morning of the twenty-first, it was the tanks of de Vernejoul's 5th DB that entered bomb-ravaged Stuttgart and clanked through the city without meeting very much opposition. The infantry, naturally moving more slowly than the armor, was further slowed down by an unyielding artillery position on a promontory called Leomberg outside the city. The 3rd RTA was blocked, but the Goumiers along with the Tirailleurs of the 4th RTT stormed the position and eliminated the enemy guns. The bulk of the infantry marched into Stuttgart that evening.

But before that, at about the same time as the French armor reached the city proper, the Tirailleurs of the 4th RTM and the Goumiers of the 4th GTM effected a junction at Deufringen, while the armor of the 3rd Regiment of Moroccan Spahis met the 1st GTM at Dagersheim, cutting off more Germans. De Lattre's plan was working.

As the tricolor rose over Stuttgart, de Lattre considered apologizing to General Devers for exceeding his orders, but then thought better of it. Certainly the American general would believe the capture of the city would be justification enough.[5] And he did. The generous Devers, whom de Lattre always thought of as an ideal comrade in arms in spite of occasional differences, congratulated de Lattre and the French army on their brilliant victory.

The next few days were devoted to mopping up (the French called it *ratissage*, "raking in") in the Stuttgart area, and most of this was done by the Goumiers in the forest zones surrounding the city. De Lattre acknowledged that Leblanc's men were "masters in these matters," and the 1st GTM was kept busy at this task until the twenty-fifth. Fifty-one hundred prisoners were "raked in" as well as all the remaining transport of the no longer existing 716th Volks-grenadier Division.

Then it was on toward Ulm on the Danube, which was of historical importance to the French as the scene of a momentous Napoleonic victory. Everyone knew the war was coming to an end, and the French had not yet been allotted an occupation zone in the conquered territory. For the French it was vital to future claims that their forces should make their mark on as much German territory as possible, so Ulm was of more than just historic and sentimental significance to de Lattre.

And then there was Sigmaringen, also on the Danube about 50 miles south of Stuttgart, significant for another reason. It was the home of the Vichy government in exile, which had fled from France in August. It was also, presumably, the residence of Marshal Pétain and his hated premier, Pierre Laval, and de Lattre hoped to capture both.

There was a problem, however. Both Sigmaringen and Ulm were not in de Lattre's territory; they were assigned to the American Seventh Army. Again that did not seem to bother the French general. He ordered elements of his 5th Armored Division, which had been fighting in the southern Black Forest not too far from Sigmaringen but still within officially assigned French territory, to proceed to that city, capture Pétain and Laval if they were still there, and then move on to Ulm. "The Americans will probably dislodge us from Ulm," de Lattre told his armored division commander. "But the French flag will have flown there."

The French troops missed Pétain and Laval at Sigmaringen, but they continued along the Danube toward Ulm, which was some forty miles outside the French zone. At Ehringen they ran into elements of the U.S. 10th Armored Division, apparently the first time Sixth Army Group realized that the French were so deeply into Seventh Army territory. Devers ordered de Lattre to withdraw; de Lattre paid no heed. He argued that the maneuver was necessary to cut off any Germans escaping from Stuttgart—even though it would seem that the 10th Armored could have prevented that.[6] The French continued on.

The first French elements reached Ulm just before nightfall of April 23. American infantry of the 44th Division arrived the next morning, followed by CCR of the 10th Armored. Soon after, French and Americans attacked from the southwest along the Danube. By midnight all resistance had ended, and the French tricolor flew over the city's old fort where the Austrians had surrendered to Napoleon in 1805. De Lattre was satisfied, and the French withdrew to their own boundaries. The Goumiers of Parlange's 4th GTM were back ten days later, performing the Tabors' acknowledged specialty of *ratissage*, mopping up in the Ulm area and along the Danube on the roads leading to the city.

Then there was another contretemps, this time involving French-occupied Stuttgart. The ruins of the city were also occupied by thousands of liberated slave laborers, including 20,000 Frenchmen. All were deliriously happy but said to be causing considerable disorder. This worried General Devers who wanted to use the road network that ran through the city for Seventh Army troop movements. Perhaps influenced by his annoyance at de Lattre's insubordinate conduct at Ulm, he again decided to change army boundaries, forcing the French out of Stuttgart, a city they had conquered and where they had now established a military government. De Lattre, of course, objected strenuously. He once again appealed to de Gaulle, who told him to stay where he was.

The rumors of disturbances in Stuttgart grew louder and more persistent, and now included stories of mass rape and plunder. Alarm bells were ringing at Sixth Army Group, and it's just possible that the people there were thinking "It's those damned Moroccans again!" Devers decided to go down to the city and see for himself.

A personal inspection on April 27 determined that the situation was not nearly as bad as the rumors indicated, was improving rapidly and had been caused by the refugees and the Germans themselves. No French troops had been involved, and the French command had been cooperating fully with the American troop movements through town. General Devers rescinded his orders regarding the French evacuation of the city, and the "Stuttgart incident" was over.

Not resting on their laurels, the French pushed on in several directions, through the hills of the Swabian Jura where they had expected to encounter heavy resistance but found little, and on down across the Danube and over the border into Austria. Further west the Goumiers of the 2nd GTM were helping to mop up what was left of the XVIII SS Army Corps, almost the last of the German Nineteenth Army that the French had been fighting since the August landings in Provence.

De Lattre's competitive spirit drove him on. Now his main desire was to reach Landeck in the Austrian Alps, which would put him in a position to link up with Allied forces in Italy. But although French troops pushed deeply into the mountains there was another inter-army dispute that complicated matters.

General Devers had issued a "warning order" to de Lattre telling him to *prepare* to take Landeck when and if the order was given. It was a "heads up" only, not an order to move, but it was all the French general needed. He immediately started his troops toward the passes that led to the Alpine town. However, Devers finally decided that Landeck was in the Seventh Army zone, and the French were blocked at every pass by American units that arrived there before them. Hearing that the Americans had not yet reached Landeck, de Lattre even sent out a patrol on borrowed skis over precipitous back roads toward the town. After an arduous twenty-five-mile trek the patrol reached

Two goumiers prepare for combat.

the Arlberg Pass where its leader made a phone call over regular commercial lines to nearby Landeck. The call was answered by an American voice—the U.S. 44th Division had just arrived.

De Lattre was still trying when the war came to a close. At the end, although he was not exactly where he had hoped to be, he could take great satisfaction that the First French Army, well into Austria and with the enemy completely destroyed, had come a very long way from the beaches of Provence.

By May 4 de Latour's men, too, had crossed the border and were now deep in the Austrian Alps. May 7 found the Goumiers alongside the 4th Moroccan Division on the heights of the Voralberg massif. That was the day of the final German surrender in Europe when the French bugles sounded the cease-fire all along the front.

For the Moroccan Tabors the long, hard-fought journey from the Atlas to the Tyrol was over. They had met the enemy and defeated him everywhere. The humiliations of the past were avenged. The Goumiers, those strange little men in the bathrobe-like *djellabas*, were finally enjoying the last laugh.

CHAPTER 6

In Retrospect

Where do the Moroccan Tabors fit into the history of World War II? They were important, certainly, in the drive on Rome, in the capture of Marseilles, in the merciless fighting in the Vosges and elsewhere. As among the last of the world's "colonial" soldiers, they perhaps belong more to a tradition dating back to the barbarian auxiliaries of the Romans rather than to the wars of the twentieth century.

On the march, in their *djellabas* and *rezzas,* with their horses and mules, they were surely circus-like in appearance. The term "tabor" is said to be of Mongol derivation, and their horsetail guidons as well as their exotic origins (and occasional pillaging) might lead some to be reminded of those barbarie raiders.

No doubt they were among the more picturesque of World War II soldiers. Historian Dan Kurzman gives a colorful description that seems to sum it all up, "They were bearded and fierce-eyed, with gleaming white teeth and plaited pigtails on their heads so Allah could pull them more easily into heaven if they were killed. They were constantly smiling, singing native songs, wanting to fight and between battles, to fornicate with any female of whatever age or inclination who happened to be around."[1]

On reflection, how valuable to the war effort were the Moroccan Goums? They were small in numbers, anywhere from 9,000 to 12,000 at any one time, all together the size of a very small division. And lightly armed—no organic artillery or armor, so they were effective mostly in a specialized way. As we have seen, that specialization was principally in the mountains. But from the Dorsales of Tunisia to the Aurunci and Lepini of Italy, the Vosges in France, the Black Forest hills in Germany and the Austrian Alps there was no better mountain infantry than the Moroccan Tabors.

Mountain fighting is perhaps the most rigorous and physically demanding of all infantry combat, particularly when attacking, as the Goumiers usually were. The defending Germans were often in relatively comfortable positions prepared long in advance. They were protected not only from artillery and small arms fire, but from the weather as well. All they had to do is look out their peepholes and pull the trigger. The attackers, on the other hand, had to scramble up the mountainside, over unknown terrain, through brush and over rocks, and frequently in horrible weather. And they had to move fast to avoid being shot before they were close enough to toss their grenades through the openings and crash into the dugout or pillbox with bayonet or knife—that is, if they hadn't collapsed of exhaustion before they made it to their objective, or hadn't stepped on a mine or been caught up in wire. And even when they were just marching in the mountains it always seemed to be up, up and up, with aching limbs and straining lungs and utter weariness.

And then there was the weather. It could be warm and dry on the plains below, but on the peaks there might be deep snow or icy rain, perpetual fog and always cold, cold winds. Just living under those conditions was difficult enough, much less fighting in them. But better than most World War II soldiers the Goumiers were able to stand these rigors, for they were born and bred in the mountains and even at home they lived much of their lives under primitive conditions. They were certainly tougher than most and were born field soldiers. A senior officer of the Tirailleurs (no mean mountain fighters themselves) describes the abilities of the Goumiers attached to the 2nd DIM in the fighting in Italy:

> The Moroccan loves the night and the mountains. Rocks, thickets and sheer crevasses, all observed in the treacherous darkness, are his best allies and over a thousand years his eyes have become accustomed to not losing their way in the gloom. He knows when to creep forward and when to wait. He knows also that there is no more fearsome weapon than that ancestral dagger which his forefathers have plunged into sentries' backs since time immemorial. Why, therefore wake the Germans before the striking of the hour of Baroud? The Germans are brave, but a brave man asleep is like a woman.[2]

But just how good were the Goumiers in the dark? There were many stories of their long night marches and nocturnal raids, of their ability to operate in the shadows. However, there is also an official report by the operations section (3rd Bureau) of the 4th Moroccan Mountain Division, made at the end of Operation Diadem, that would seem to contradict this. It concluded that the Goumiers showed "a manifest reticence in regard to operations at night where they frequently lost contact; the tabors in general tended to halt their action in the evening, if possible, passing a part of their night comfortably in their bivouac to complete their mission at daylight."[3] But remember, this judgment was made by officers of the Tirailleurs, regulars who never seemed quite comfortable with the informality and perhaps even slackness, of the Goums.

But even the Goumiers' own officers were sometimes not sure of the tribesmens' reliability. At one time Guillaume himself reported to Juin:

> The goums . . . even more than the Tirailleurs . . . have retained intact the qualities and the weaknesses of their race; indisputable valour in war, but unreliability under stress; an offensive spirit exalted by success, but

> soon dissipated by failure; an innate courage in infantry combat, but a tendency to become unsettled in the face of modern weapons; a peasant hardiness and an innate sense of ground, but an aversion to hard work and discipline.[4]

That, in a nutshell, is a picture of the Goumiers, warts and all.

But perhaps not quite all. The Goums were prepared to live off the land, and they didn't particularly care whose land it was. As mentioned earlier, they were often seen on the march leading goats and sheep, not mascots but rations on the hoof. It is unlikely that these were issued along with their American "C" and "K" rations, and even less likely that they were purchased.

And then there were the brutal rapes, which the French officers punished with equal brutality, shooting and sometimes hanging the offenders. The Italian peasants suffered and complained, but it was not until the advent of additional French cadres that the worst of these offenses were finally stopped.

Nevertheless, for every minus there was a plus. One of the military virtues of the tribesmen was their extreme mobility. They traveled light. While the Tirailleurs were burdened with heavy American packs, blankets, mess kits and all the other paraphernalia of regular soldiers, the Goumiers often carried most of their possessions in a musette bag. They packed their machine guns and mortars on their ever-present mules and slept in their *djellabas*.

If the value of the Goums was suspect in some quarters, so was the military opinions of the senior French officers. When the French Expeditionary Corps first came to Italy, the British and American high command paid scant attention to the views of its leaders. The original plan was for the British Eighth Army, greatly reinforced and highly mechanized, to play the main role in the spring offensive, charging its way through the

German lines into the Liri Valley and then on to Rome. Juin took one look at the mountains, and had his doubts.

The French commander had definite ideas (shared by Guillaume and the other FEC leaders with mountain fighting experience in Morocco) of going around the main German defenses at Cassino and passing through the less heavily defended but extremely difficult terrain to the south. He didn't approve of the Allies' costly direct attacks on the strongest part of the enemy's defenses. His idea was to attack the weaker sectors and keep on going. *Zidou l'goudem*!

But many in the Allied high command did not agree. They remembered the struggles of the poorly equipped French army in Tunisia, and in spite of the early FEC successes in Italy, they didn't feel that the French forces were yet ready for modern warfare. It was not until those sensational gains of the Tirailleurs and Goumiers in the northern part of the line in January were fully realized that the British and Americans began to give the French their due.

Even then, in the original plans for Diadem, the FEC was given only so much to do. Juin was dissatisfied. He had a better idea, an attack on three axes—British, French and American—including the drive through the Aurunci, which he presented to both the British and American staffs. There was much head shaking—the mountains were impassable, the French couldn't pull it off—and perhaps there was still the shadow of France's 1940 defeat hanging over the conference tables. But Juin's ideas were eventually, if reluctantly, incorporated in the final plan—and we've seen how well they worked in the drive on Rome.

The manner in which the French swept through the Aurunci impressed everyone, allies and enemy alike. There was heroism enough to go around in all camps in the Italian campaign, but the French seemed to be able to pull off spectacular acts of gallantry with a theatricality that made them stand out. The junior officers and non-coms of the Goums in particular showed outstanding leadership, for the tribesmen had to be led by example. One hears again and again of lieutenants and captains under heavy fire simply standing up and walking toward the enemy. *Zidou l'goudem,* forward and keep going! And the Goumiers would leap to their feet and follow. Obviously, these tactics led to many casualties among the leaders—but they also led to victory.

The terms *élan, panache, audace* have always been associated with the French military, and the officers of the tabors were no exception. Guillaume was continually reminding his people that the world was watching them, that they had to make up for previous defeats and humiliations and that their actions reflected on France and the French army in general and on the Moroccan Tabors in particular. Forward, always forward! There is no doubt that the junior officers took these exhortations to heart. That they were going home, returning to "the sacred soil of France," redeeming their country's honor—all these thoughts played a large part in so many of their courageous acts. And though none of these reasons really applied to their Berber followers, the Goumiers caught the spirit and they followed their officers into battle with equal fervor. The tribesmen had their own idea of honor.

Language barriers seemed to play only a small part in leadership difficulties among the Goums. As they moved into France, increasing casualties necessitated more replacements, and among the junior officers these tended to be reservists. They were not all originally from North Africa although they had been processed through the 22nd Tabor, the replacement unit for the Goums. The percentage of old-timers, the *ancièns* of the *Service des Affaires Indigenes,* decreased, but the newcomers picked up enough Arabic or *Chleuh* (the common name for the Berber languages)[5] to make themselves understood. And by this time most of the tribesmen could speak Arabic and a good bit of French besides. Most ordinarily used phrases such as *ach kim*? (who goes there?) and *grib*! (pass!) were spoken in the native tongues of Morocco. But as their leaders pointed out, all the Goumiers really had to know was *Zidou*! Forward!

Tabor officers attempted to maintain the customs of the tribesmen as much as possible, and one of these customs was the *chikaya*. This was a kind of periodic meeting, similar to the councils of most tribal countries, where the leaders listen to the grievances of their people and try to answer their questions. Since the Goumiers were largely unschooled, the questions were often naive and sometimes unanswerable. Usually, however, they were fairly simple. Typical was the Goumier of the 1st GTM who, when he heard they were going to Corsica (in preparation for Operation Dragoon), asked if Corsica was anywhere near Paris. He had heard his officers speak of a wonderland called Paris, and he wanted to see it for himself. He had never heard of Corsica. Yes, his lieutenant told him with a homesick sigh, Corsica was nearer to Paris than where they were now in southern Italy—but not near enough.[6]

As the Goums moved closer to the German homeland, they ran into an ever increasing panoply of enemy weapons. When they entered the line in Tunisia, they had never before faced concentrated artillery fire, for the dissident tribesmen they had fought against in the days of pacification had no artillery. Their first encounter with cannon fire in Tunisia was terrifying. It was even worse in Italy and France where the enemy had a wider variety of guns—and more of them. There, in addition to the dreaded 88s they had known in North Africa, they met the six-barreled *Nebelwerfer*, the so-called "screaming meemie" with its fearful whistling shreik, as well as a frighteningly large assortment of other artillery and mortars. The post-Italy critique had declared the Goumiers "perhaps a bit more sensitive to heavy artillery fire and mines than the regulars,"[7] but familiarity breeds contempt, and by the end of the war the tribesmen had become as used to artillery fire as only veteran infantry can be.

As for mines, the Germans used every kind of personnel mine imaginable, from the "schu" mine designed to blow off the victim's foot to the "bouncing Betty" that rose several feet in the air before it exploded. The Goumiers were as wary of these horrors as anyone else, but they learned to deal with them. Although some observers maintained that they misused mine detectors, General de Lattre himself commented on their bravery and skill in lifting mines by hand in the Haguenau Forest and the Siegfried Line.[8]

German tanks continued to be a problem throughout the war, and the Goumiers never learned to deal with them satisfactorily. One reason the tribesmen preferred to operate in the most rugged of mountain terrain was that tanks would seldom venture there. However, the Moroccans were quite comfortable when they were called upon to be part of infantry-tank teams, in cooperation with Allied armor—just as long as the tanks were on their side.

By the end of the war, the men of the Tabors were adept at most forms of infantry combat, but they were particularly deadly at hand-to-hand combat and what was known as *nettoyage*, cleaning up areas overlooked by quickly advancing friendly troops, usually armor or truck borne infantry. They were considered specialists in these techniques, and they enjoyed the game. The French officers considered this somewhat dangerous duty almost as a rest, and called it a *periode sportif.* The German soldiers found it not so sporting; it was difficult indeed to hide from the determined tribesmen. At the very end of the war, as the enemy units disintegrated, this *chasse de l'homme* became even more important, and the Goums were kept busy rounding up prisoners right up until peace was officially declared.

Even before this period, another story had surfaced about the Goums. It was said that the Goumiers were "selling" their prisoners to less fortunate Allied soldiers who had captured none of their own, and that there was an established price list of POWs according to rank.[9] But once again the story was denied, and like many such tales about the Moroccans, it is impossible to prove or disprove.

The cavalry of the Tabors, the mounted reconnaissance platoons, existed to the end, although in reduced numbers. The Moroccans were proud of their horsemanship and every country féte at home featured a "fantasia," a spectacle of equestrian skill ending with a wild charge, the riders firing their ancient weapons in the air. These skills transferred to the military proved useful throughout the war; the mounted Goumiers were invaluable in scouting and patrolling where the terrain prevented the use of motor vehicles. Their mounts were "Barbs," the Barbary Coast horses of North Africa, tough as the rocks of their native mountains and as accustomed to hardship as the Goumiers themselves. The saddles were the equally rugged but extremely bulky and uncomfortable Arab affairs, the kind used throughout the Maghreb.

The officers of the Tabors also found horses useful since jeeps were scarce, and even when available much of the countryside where the Goums operated was "unjeepable," passable only to horses, mules and men. But the Frenchmen used the more comfortable army officers' saddle rather than the Goumiers' native counterpart.

If one remembers that the original Moroccan Goums of 1907 were all horsemen, it would seem that the reduction in the size of its cavalry was a major change. During the wartime years, however, there were many other alterations in the tactics and techniques and, indeed, the very missions of the tribal warriors. As we have seen, before the war most of the Goums were basically local militia raised to police their own territories and act as scouts for the French army pacification columns that entered their remote areas. As "auxiliaries" they essentially lived the life of a normal tribesman, sharing the mudbrick fortress homes of their walled villages, or living in their black tents or semi-permanent huts as they looked after their herds of cattle, sheep or goats. Some were subsistence farmers, living on the meager crops of their small holdings and storing grain in the village granaries for future trading. Some bred, raised and traded donkeys, mules and horses.

The first notable change in their lives might have come with the visit of the local recruiting officer, and it was not much of a change at that. The prospective recruit most likely knew the recruiter, for he was probably a French officer of the *Service des Affaires Indigenes* and the commander of the local Goum. Like an American National Guard company commander, the Goum officer was responsible for recruiting and maintaining the strength of his own unit, an added responsibility the regular officer did not have.

The men of the local Goum were likely to be brothers, cousins or uncles of the new recruit, and if not family, the Goumiers were sure to be friends and acquaintances from the same area. Even the change into uniform was not too severe, for the *djellaba* and turban were similar to his civilian dress. And if he were married, he lived at home and might even want to bring his wife along on campaign, a practice that later helped convince the German armistice commissioners that the Goumiers couldn't possibly be real soldiers—at least not in the correct Prussian mold.

The discipline, although it might seem severe to the independent-minded Berber, was not all that tough, and the training, the small unit tactics in the mountain terrain, was not very different from the harsh everyday life of the Berber mountaineer. The very few French officers and non-coms overseeing the Goums of that prewar era had a laissez-faire attitude; they knew they had a good thing in the natural warrior abilities of their men and they were not about to spoil it by trying to make them into regulars. During this period there were numerous changes in organization—some Goums operated together, some separately, some purely infantry, others mixed with cavalry. And among the fifty-seven Goums active throughout Morocco at the beginning of 1939, two actually had a platoon of *méharistes,* Goumiers mounted on camels—very practical in the Saharan regions.

The Goums were pretty much organized in this informal way when war came in 1939. In May 1940 when those twelve Goums were hastily thrown together to form the *1st Groupe de Supplétifs Marocains* and sent to the Tunisian border to fight the Italians, they were still formed in that irregular manner. It wasn't until the armistice came in June and the Goums were once again separated and sent back to their original depots that the idea was born to reorganize and train them secretly for the *opérations classiques* of a real army. This was a radical change that transformed them from policemen into soldiers, although the Germans never realized it. In fact, the armistice commissioners were led to believe that the large numbers of mountain tribesmen that were beginning to appear at newly opened recruiting stations were being signed up as laborers for a series of contemplated public works projects. The Germans never caught on until the *djellabas* showed up later on the battlefields of Tunisia with machine guns and mortars and a pretty good idea of modern infantry tactics.

A study of the Moroccan Goums would not be complete without mention of their long-suffering companions, the tough, patient mules who were so often at their side. The mules were an absolute necessity in the mountains. They not only carried all supplies up to the forward troops, but were just as useful in getting the wounded down. While the art of mule skinning had all but died out in the British and American armies and had to be learned all over again in the mountains of Italy and France, it was second nature to the Moroccans. Unlike their allies, who too often had to scramble around for local animals, the Goumiers brought most of their pack animals with them. And on those rare occasions when they had to rely on the locals for remounts, they were more willingly given to the French forces than to the others. The Moroccans knew how to handle the animals, too, for mules and horses were as common in their native Atlas as automobiles on an American highway.

But animal transportation had its weaknesses. The mules were slow, feeding and watering was always a problem, carrying capacity was limited (around 150 pounds, depending on the animal) and they were extremely vulnerable to shellfire. Many, many were killed by enemy action. Accidents took their toll, too, for even a sure footed mule could slip while being hurried along a narrow trail and plunge over a cliff or into a crevasse. In spite of these drawbacks, no troops could operate without them in the remote mountains where the Goums did their best work.

When the mules themselves had to be transported long distances, there were several ways of doing this. For years past mules and horses had been conveyed by rail in the famous "40 and 8" (forty men or eight horses) freight cars, and in World War II it was discovered that in a pinch they could also be conveyed in the American 2.5-ton cargo truck. Loading and unloading could be accomplished with makeshift ramps or simply by backing the truck into a convenient hillside. Of course, horses and mules have been transported by sea on the decks of ships for centuries, but in this war a better way was found—the landing ship, tank. During the war thousands of mules were shipped across the Mediterranean on the tank decks of 1sts, which were much easier to load and unload than transports.

U.S. Navy landing ships were also useful for another unique purpose. The Moroccan Goumiers were perhaps the only soldiers of World War II who brought their own women with them. Back in Morocco they were used to taking their women on campaign, and when the rape problem appeared in Italy, the French authorities decided to bring Moroccan women to Europe and establish them in rear area rest camps that were set aside exclusively for Goumiers. Passing one of these camps you might see a colorfully clad Moroccan girl, all bangles and bracelets and rings, and some with a traditional facial tattoo, listening to an off-duty Goumier strumming a native stringed instrument and chanting a Berber love song.

There were other aspects of a Goumier's life that did not seem to fit in with the picture of a fierce, merciless warrior. At times an unexpected tenderness rose to the surface. The concern and sadness that overtook the 3rd Tabor when their leader, Commandant Méric, was severely wounded during the Vosges campaign was a case in point. When he unexpectedly recovered and returned to the Tabor, he was joyously greeted as a *marabout*, a Muslim saint, and the happiness and love of his Goumiers was obviously genuine.[10]

Again, when refugees from villages torched by the Germans stumbled into the lines of the 2nd GTM, they were received with the utmost sympathy. The Goumiers packed the meager family belongings on their mules and led them to safety, sometimes carrying the children in their arms. When one Goumier was offered a monetary reward, he refused it saying, "It is for France." That these men, so often accused of indiscriminate pillage and worse, could act in this unlikely manner seems remarkable. It adds to the mysteries surrounding the Berbers of the Atlas.

Hardly less of a mystery was the "Frenchification" of the Goumiers after they had served in France for a while. According to Captain Pierre Lyautey, the Goumier liaison officer whose duties took him all over the front lines among the Goums and the 3rd DIA, the Goumier's attitude toward French civilians had become one of "politesse and oriental gallantry." They began to admire all things French, and some of them even adopted French surnames. At one point Lyautey's own orderly, Hamou, began calling himself "Pierre."[11]

Of course the Frenchmen in the Tabors had, in reverse, long since taken on the airs of a Moroccan. They wore the *djellaba* over their uniform, the badge on their *kepi* was the crescent of Islam, and they peppered their speech with Arabic and Berber phrases. Even their official code names were of North African origin. For instance, Leblanc's 1st GTM was known as *Hallali*, de Latour's 2nd GTM was *Minaret*, while du Biest's 3rd GTM answered to *Bled*. By extension, each of those French leaders was himself called by the distinctly oriental *nom de guerre* of his unit. All this shared culture added up to a special swagger among the officers and promoted a high morale throughout the Goums.

At only one period was morale in the Tabors noticeably low, and at the time that was an attitude shared by virtually all the Allied troops in Alsace-Lorraine. It was at the height of the Vosges campaign, when the heavy snowfalls, punctuated by incessant icy rains, deep mud and overflowing streams plus increased battle casualties and weather-related illnesses caused a universal gloom. Everyone was cold and wet all the time. Captain Lyautey, originally a native of the Lorraine country where the fighting was going on, recalls a remark made to him by a rain-soaked Colonel de Latour as they both were being pelted by a frigid downpour, "*Ah, Pierre, votre Lorraine, quel pays de merde!*"[12]

There were other problems, too. Supplies were not getting through, and the Goumiers were virtually in rags. De Lattre worried about the morale situation and appealed to higher headquarters, citing the shortage of manpower and supplies—with little result. But with the approach of spring and the improvement in both the weather and the supply predicament, the smiles returned to the faces of the Goumiers, and the morale crisis was over. Spirits were at their highest when spring flowers blossomed, the Tabors crossed the Rhine and the Boche were on the run.

The joys of victory, however, had a price, a very high price for the Tabors. The final casualty figures as calculated by the French Army Historical Service, killed, wounded and missing are: 1st GTM, 2,196; 2nd GTM, 2,977; 3rd GTM, 2,676; 4th

GTM, 3,157. These figures are approximate. In the carnage of war, identification of the dead is often difficult and casualty lists are sometimes inaccurate. Numbers are juggled, records are lost, but the figures can give at least some idea of the sacrifices made.

All in all the World War II service of the Moroccan Goumiers was neatly summed up in *Le Chant des Tabors,* a song written in French after the great adventure was over. Here's a rough translation of the first verse

> Zidou l'goudem, Zidou l'goudem
> Hear the song of the Tabors
> March on, keep going no matter what
> Up until the end, up until death
> Crying "Zidou l'goudem!"
> That's the hard law of the Tabor

It then goes on for six more verses (see Appendix III) recalling the exploits of the Goums from Tunisia to the Danube. It ends up with

> They will sing, one thing is sure,
> For one-hundred years and many more
> Of the exploits and adventures
> Of those who fought so many battles.
> Goumier, in your monk's robe,
> You must now go back to your tribe.

Some did go back to their tribes, while others elected to stay in the tabors. And many others, wrapped in their *djellabas,* remained forever in the military cemeteries of Europe.

Epilogue

The Goumiers, when they returned to Morocco, found it a different land from the one they had left. The spirit of independence, always bright, was now burning with a new intensity. The political pot was stirring everywhere in Africa and Asia, and most of the old colonial powers were loosening their grip on their colonies and "protectorates"—but the French were determined to hold on to theirs.

As the Berbers of the Tabors were discharged from the army and returned to their villages, farms and herds, they found that they themselves had changed. They were no longer the primitive innocents of another day. They had seen something of the world and had gained a degree of sophistication they never had before. With it had come a realization of their own political power. The tribes were once again restive, but the freedom the Berbers now sought was less from the French colonialists than it was from the sultan and his Makhzen.

The party of independence, the Istiqlal, allied with Sultan Mohammed ben Yusuf, defied the French authorities and demanded full independence. The very conservative mountain Berbers, on the other hand, preferred the old ways and supported the southern leader, El Glawi, the pasha of Marrakesh, the sultan's rival. They asked for the removal of the sultan. When that was not forthcoming, a huge flood of tribesmen poured down from the mountains on horse and on foot and threatened the major cities. The sultan refused to formally abdicate, but went into exile and was replaced by Mohammed ben Arafa, a compromise the Berbers accepted. The tribesmen went back to their mountains, and although the original sultan eventually returned to the throne and Morocco gained its independence under him in 1956, the Berbers had found their voice in Moroccan affairs.[1]

In the meanwhile the Tabors were still a part of the French army and up until independence continued to fight for France. They served throughout the French phase of the war in Indochina from 1948 until the end in 1954.

After the war General Augustin-Léon Guillaume continued his distinguished career. In 1945 he was named military attaché in Moscow, an important and appropriate appointment for a man with his background in intelligence. Then in 1947 and 1948 he had two postings as adjutant, one to the inspector general of the French army and the other to the commander of French troops in Germany. The latter assignment put him in line for his next position, when in 1950 he was appointed chief of all French occupation forces in Germany.

But as prestigious as these jobs were, the emotional peak of his career must have been in 1951 when he was named resident commissioner general of France in Morocco and inspector general of all forces, land, sea and air in French North Africa. The great Auroch (the wartime code name for the commandant of Goums) had come home to his beloved Morocco, to his Goums, to the scenes of his earliest triumphs and the base for his many military successes. His final and most notable appointment (although it might have seemed an anticlimax after the Moroccan assignment) came in 1954 when he became chief of staff of all French forces, a position comparable to our chairman of the joint chiefs. He retired to the reserves in 1956 and died at his home in Guillestre in the *Hautes Alpes* in 1983.

Two other Tabor officers heard from after the war were Colonel Boyer de Latour, who commanded the 2nd GTM throughout the conflict, and Colonel Parlange, leader of the 4th GTM in the final battles in Germany. Both later became generals and served with distinction, de Latour in the difficult times in Vietnam and Parlange in the Algerian conflict.[2] De Latour later suffered a degree of notoriety when he appeared as a witness for the defense in a widely publicized trial involving a military plot against the government in 1961.

Other French officers who had influenced (or been influenced by) the Goums in World War II rose to even greater prominence after the war. General Juin became a marshal of France (the army's highest rank) and was chief of staff of the armed forces before Guillaume. He later became head of Allied Land Forces, Central Europe, an integral part of NATO—and thus became a world figure. He died in 1957.

General Jean de Lattre de Tassigny became even more widely known after the war as the one general who ever seemed to have a handle on the situation in the French phase of the Vietnam war. He went to Indochina at a low point in the fortunes of the French army there, and had accepted the command only with the proviso that he would be high commissioner as well as the military commander-in-chief.

When de Lattre arrived on the scene the French had just taken a severe beating from the Vietminh, the Vietnamese rebels, at Cao Bang and had lost some 3,000 killed or captured. Cao Bang was a complete disaster, but displayed the Goums at the height of their mountaineering effectiveness—and, according to some, at the worst of fear-induced panic.

The town of Cao Bang was a French outpost on the Chinese border of Tonkin, the northernmost province of Vietnam. It was surrounded by massive fog-shrouded mountain peaks covered with almost impenetrable jungle. And hidden in that hostile terrain were thousands of well-armed Vietminh soldiers, ready to pounce.

The poorly informed French headquarters many miles away ordered the garrison commander, Foreign Legion Colonel Charton, to evacuate the town, sending as many civilians as possible out by air. He was then to march down Route Coloniale (RC) 4 south to Thatke, another outpost town but one more heavily defended. At the same time a French column was to be sent out from Thatke to meet and strengthen Charton's people and escort them back to the comparative safety of Thatke.

Colonel Charton's column had along with it about 500 civilian refugees, while the military contingent consisted of a battalion of the Foreign Legion, a group of native partisans, and the 3rd Moroccan Tabor under Commandant Chergé. They started out in good order and with a confident air, but they were soon being sniped at by hidden Vietminh. It didn't bother them much. The Moroccans were at their cheerful best, routing out the Viet pockets and taking turns with the Legion in leading the column or scouting along the mountainous flanks of RC 4.

The relief column out of Thatke led by artillery Colonel Lepage consisted of a battalion of Foreign Legion paratroopers, the 8th RTM and two Tabors, the 11th and the 1st, under Commandant Delcros and Captain Faugas respectively. They started out not quite as confidently as Charton's column, for the Legionnaires looked down on the Moroccans as they did on virtually all other troops, especially "natives," and they had absolutely no respect whatever for Colonel Lepage, a mere artilleryman.

Exactly what happened next is clouded by the fog of war, but both columns were attacked by huge masses of Viets—and both columns were decimated. The battered survivors finally rendezvoused in the jungle near Dongke, and a handful, both Legionnaires and Goumiers, made it back to Thatke. It was then that the stories of Moroccan panic and disgrace were told—by the Legionnaires.

The report was that under intense attack the Goumiers of the 3rd Tabor ran from their ridgeline positions without firing a shot and disappeared into the jungle. It was also said that when the remnants of the two French columns met, the Moroccans from Thatke were in a state of absolute panic, firing their weapons at nothing in particular and running about wildly.

But there were other tales, too. Another Legion survivor described the Goumiers at the very end, "Some completely surrounded Moroccans charged, singing a battle chant until they were all killed."[3] That sounds more like it.

With the arrival of de Lattre, the French troops, whose morale was at an all-time low, were galvanized into action. With his usual energy, the new commander shook things up from top to bottom. He withdrew troops from the south, which at the moment was comparatively quiet, and threw them into action in the north, and in a two day battle at Vinh Yen in January 1951, defeated the Vietminh regulars of General Vo Nguyen Giap. He organized mobile patrols and built a string of blockhouses around the vital Red River delta area, which included Hanoi and Haiphong. And in another battle with the Vietminh at Dong Trieu, he once again defeated the troops of General Giap. Things were definitely looking up in Indochina when personal tragedy struck. His son, Lieutenant Bernard de Lattre, was killed in action at Ninh Binh. The general did not live long after him. Jean de Lattre de Tassigny died of cancer in January 1952, and was posthumously made a marshal of France.

From then on the war did not go well for the French, eventually leading to their last great gamble in Indochina. This was at Dien Bien Phu, an "air-land" base that had been established in a valley far behind the Vietminh lines in the remote mountainous wilds of northwest Vietnam, near the Laotian border. It was garrisoned by a combined force of Foreign Legionnaires, Moroccan and Algerian Tirailleurs, French and Vietnamese paratroopers, infantry, engineers, artillery and armor, as well as local T'ai tribesmen. It had been organized by paratroopers and was being supplied and reinforced entirely by air.[4]

Sixty miles to the north, the Goumiers of the 2nd Moroccan Tabor were part of the garrison of Lai Chai, a regional center with a small airfield, now threatened by approaching Vietminh. It was decided to evacuate the area, and the Goumiers were flown down to Dien Bien Phu. They had to leave their mules behind, however, and some 400 animals (including those of other units) were loose in the abandoned town. They would fall into enemy hands; apparently the Goumiers were too soft-hearted to shoot them. The 2nd Tabor was now part of the Dien Bien Phu garrison.

There were two reasons for establishing this base out in the middle of nowhere. The first was to distract the Viets from their continuing attacks in the Red River delta, which were seriously hurting the French. The other was to create a "mooring" from which the French forces could venture out to patrol in Vietminh territory, gather intelligence and destroy any enemy units they ran into.[5]

One of the earliest of these missions was planned for December 1953, the purpose of which was to reach Sop Nao on the Laotion side of the border to contact a French column marching through Laos to meet it. There was no real military reason for this particular task, except to prove that Dien Bien Phu was not as isolated from other French forces as the French public may have thought. To that end the press corps had been brought to Sop Nao to witness and photograph the meeting of the two columns.

The task of the paratroopers marching from Dien Bien Phu under Lieutenant-Colonel Langlais[6] was not an easy one. It was through some of the toughest jungle and mountain terrain in the world, over 6,000-foot cliffs and through swift running streams—but the march was easier than that of the forces coming from Laos. That column consisted of the 5th Battalion of Laotian Chasseurs and the 5th Moroccan Tabor, the latter commanded by Commandant Coquelet. The force was code named "Ardeche,"[7] and its overall commander was Commandant Vaudrey. These troops had marched 200 miles across.

Laos, and had not only the horrible jungle terrain to contend with, but the continual harassment of Communist Pathet Lao guerrillas as well. But even stronger opposition was met at Muong Khoua, an important river crossing not far from their goal, where a battalion of Vietminh Regiment 148 was dug in and waiting.

When the Goumiers discovered that they had run into a hornets' nest, they made their usual painstaking reconnaissance and found their entrenched enemy to be well equipped with machine guns and mortars and the area thoroughly mined. The Moroccans did not let that deter them. Old hands at mountain fighting, they soon took the hills overlooking the enemy position. Although the Viets were outnumbered, they were skilled and determined, and it took the Goumiers and Chasseurs more than a day of hard fighting to pry them out of their positions. That night the remnants of the battered Vietminh battalion fled into the jungle. The French forces marched on.

Just a few miles short of Sop Nao was the village of Nga Na Son with its tiny airfield, which had been made completely useless by the Communists. While the Chasseurs pushed on to Sop Nao, the 5th Tabor became combat engineers to repair the airstrip at Nga Na Son. They set up a defensive perimeter and worked all night with air-dropped picks and shovels to fill the holes and level the mounds of earth the Viets had thrown across the runway. The next day Colonel Christian de Castries, the dashing, aristocratic new commander at Dien Bien Phu landed in his little observation plane to witness the meeting of the Laotians with the paratroopers at Sop Nao. It all made little sense, even to the Moroccans, for they would later realize that their fight with the Vietminh at Muong Khoua was one of the last successes of French arms in Indochina.

Back at Dien Bien Phu there was increasing Vietminh activity, with enemy units drawing ever nearer. On December 30 the 2nd Tabor started out on a search and destroy mission and less than four miles to the south ran into a strong Communist force. In the battle that followed, the Moroccans suffered heavy losses. Not long after, the exhausted Tabor was transferred out of the base and replaced by fresher troops. The last Goumiers to serve at Dien Bien Phu, they were the lucky ones.

Things continued to go downhill for the French, and after they were defeated in the battle of Dien Bien Phu in 1954 they withdrew from Indochina. Their defeat in the far east had a chain effect in North Africa. Many of the returning Moroccan troops had been infected with the virus of independence, encouraged by their Vietnamese conquerors, and their voices were added to the others at home clamoring for freedom from colonial rule. It all ended in 1956 when Morocco was granted its cherished goal, and the French withdrew.

At almost the same time Tunisia became independent, leaving Algeria the last state in the Maghreb to remain under French control. The French authorities were determined to keep it that way. What followed then was a tragic war in which the old comrades-in-arms of World War II fought against each other. Most of the senior French officers had been leaders of the Arab and Berber troops in the war against Germany, while many of the rebels had learned their trade as soldiers under those same officers. The rebellion started in 1954, and when the smoke cleared in 1962 and Algeria was free, its first president was a man named Ahmed ben Bella who had been a sergeant in the 7th Regiment of Algerian Tirailleurs fighting for France in World War II.

According to the French Army Historical Service, the Goums did not serve in the Algerian War. But New York Times correspondent Michael K. Clark, reporting on French reverses in early fighting in the Aurès region wrote, "The French military position seems to have improved slightly in February [1955] with the arrival of Moroccan *Tabors*, native troops noted for their mobility and toughness."[8] That was just about the last to be heard of the Goums fighting for France. The next year brought independence to Morocco, and the Tabors marched out of the French service forever.

There is a bizarre postscript to this story. The returning GIs of World War II brought a few tales of these strange warriors back to America, but these seem to have been quickly forgotten. Some years later, however, a "realistic" war movie came out about the conflict in Italy, starring popular actress Sophia Loren. In the most notable scene the heroine is raped by "African" soldiers—and there they are, the Goumiers, accurately pictured on the silver screen, striped *djellabas*, turbans, French officers and all. So in America if the Goumiers are ever remembered, it may not be as World War II heroes, as they surely deserve, but as brutal, leering villains, as perhaps at times they were.

Today Morocco is a tourists' paradise. It offers pleasant weather, sensational scenery, colorful market places complete with acrobats and snake charmers, luxury hotels, even a Club Med. From the balcony of the posh Mamounia Hotel in Marrakesh can be seen the snow-capped peaks of the Atlas. Beyond that, travel agencies offer expensive "cultural tours" where, if you don't mind roughing it, you can visit the land of the mountain Berbers, still remote and isolated. If you want to witness the seasonal mass marriage ceremonies of the Ait Haddidou, one of the last tribes to surrender to the French, you have to travel by Land Rover and then by foot or mule to reach their villages. But, the travel brochures warn, the sanitary facilities on the trip are sometimes not all they should be.

In these remote areas of the sparsely populated Atlas, a land where television has not yet penetrated, tribal storytellers still recite their traditional tales as they have since time immemorial. Although internecine warfare is pretty much a thing of the past in these mountains, the stories are still about battles, blood feuds and cattle raids of another era. Now a new chapter has been added, a stirring epic of mountain warriors, the Berber heroes who fought and conquered an enemy called "the Boche" in strange lands far away. The listeners are invariably enchanted, and in these hills the story tellers have made the Moroccan Tabors immortal.

APPENDIX I

The Uniforms

Since the Goums were irregular troops, their uniforms tended to be somewhat irregular too, particularly before they were rearmed and equipped by the Americans.

The most important item of apparel was the *djellaba*, the long woolen cloak that distinguished the man as a Goumier. This might be of varying patterns, according to the area from which his particular tabor was recruited. There were, in general, two distinct designs. The first was a dark one with alternating black and brown vertical bands, separated by a narrow white stripe. The other was a light grayish tan with what might be called "pinstripes." Under certain conditions both patterns provided excellent camouflage, especially when dirtied up by field service. Each *djellaba* had a capacious hood called a *khoub*. These gave the Goumiers a monk-like and somehow threatening appearance, and when not in use as protection from the weather could be employed as an additional carryall.

Another useful item was the *shesh*, a long khaki scarf that could be wound around the neck and face against weather and dust and was often worn as a turban. In Africa the Goumiers were also issued a *gandoura*, a lightweight khaki smock, and *serouals*, baggy, midleg Arab pantaloons. Mounted officers wore the *gandoura* with boots and breeches, while the dismounted French cadre favored the cool, voluminous, ankle-length *serouals* of the Saharan companies, with sandals.

These comfortable native leather sandals were the regular footwear of all the Goumiers, and in exceptionally cold weather

1. This French captain is wearing the lightweight *gandoura*, popular in North Africa, over riding breeches, but his riding boots have either been completely worn out or are being saved for a more important occasion. The high knee-socks are a common replacement for scarce boots or *puttees*. 2. This is the ordinary dress of the goumier before the Tabors were rearmed by the Americans. He's wearing the typical black *rezza* (turban) and dark, striped *djellaba*. His ammunition pouches and belt are of French army origin. He wears sandals over bare feet. The woolen leggings are called *tighiwines*. 3. It's all American equipment for this latter-day goumier, from his World War I helmet to his GI shoes and leggings. His web ammunition belt, canteen, and Model 1903 Springfield rifle are U.S. Army issue, but his light-colored *djellaba* is strictly Moroccan.

were worn with heavy woolen socks. A commonly seen variant was a sort of woolen legging, footless, and also worn with sandals. And often the Goumiers preferred to go barefoot, as we have seen in General de Lattre's description of the approach march to Marseilles. With American equipment and uniforms they also received GI shoes and canvas leggings.

The Goumiers' everyday headress was the *rezza*, long strands of black cotton, intertwined and wound around the head, turban fashion. Also worn on occasion was a knit skullcap woven in a traditional Moroccan design. There was considerable variety in the steel helmets issued to the Tabors. Those supplied by the Americans were of the flat World War I type, while some Goums received the French 1915 model with an Islamic crescent insignia on the front. A few Goumiers could eventually be seen in the more modern U.S. bowl shaped helmet with plastic liner, but these were probably picked up on the battlefield rather than official issue. In the Tunisian campaign the Tabors wore the old-fashioned French leather belt and ammunition pouches, but later were supplied with American web equipment, which they wore throughout the rest of the war.

The uniforms of the officers were as varied as that of their men. The poverty of the French army at the time it fought with the Allies in Tunisia was evident, and the Tabors were no exception. Carefully preserved but well-worn uniforms never seemed quite complete. If mounted officers had leather riding boots or puttees, they often showed heavy scuffs, scratches and other signs of wear, and when completely worn out simply could not be replaced. When this happened they wore high knee socks with their riding breeches. Popular headgear was the *bonnet de police*, the French version of the overseas cap.

In those transitional stages before complete American equipment was issued, the French cadres in the Goums were dressed in whatever bits and pieces of uniform they could find. In Corsica the author remembers a conversation with a young lieutenant who was wearing British battle dress, probably picked up in Tunisia where some of the Goums fought under the British First Army. His sky blue *kepi* with crescent badge was characteristic of French North African troops, but he wore his jacket open to display a scarlet vest of oriental design in startling contrast to the rest of his sombre military attire. Also seen on the streets of Bastia, among other strange uniforms, was a Tabor captain in a plain olive drab *djellaba* that must surely have been fashioned from American G.I. blankets.

Of course, all French officers and NCOs of the Goums at most times wore over their uniforms the authentic Moroccan *djellaba*, of which they were justifiably proud. Add to that the popular walking cane and the occasional swagger stick and you have, in spite of the somewhat worn and shabby uniform, an officer with a debonair, exotic, but always soldierly appearance.

APPENDIX II

Troop List of Moroccan Tabors, World War II

Headquarters (General Guillaume, Colonel Hogard)
- Headquarters Goum
- Service Goum
- 22nd Instruction Tabor

1st Group of Moroccan Tabors (Colonel Leblanc)
- Headquarters and Service Goum
- 2nd Tabor (Headquarters, 51st, 61st, 62nd Goums)
- 3rd Tabor (Headquarters, 4th, 65th, 101st Goums)
- 12th Tabor (Headquarters, 12th, 63rd, 64th Goums)

2nd Group of Moroccan Tabors (Colonel Boyer de Latour)
- Headquarters and Service Goum
- 1st Tabor (Headquarters, 58th, 59th, 60th Goums)
- 6th Tabor (Headquarters, 8th, 11th, 73rd Goums)
- 15th Tabor (Headquarters, 39th. 47th, 74th Goums)

3rd Group of Moroccan Tabors (Colonel Massiet du Biest)
- Headquarters and Service Goum
- 9th Tabor (Headquarters, 81st, 82nd, 83rd Goums)
- 10th Tabor (Headquarters, 84th, 85th, 86th Goums)
- 17th Tabor (Headquarters, 14th, 18th, 22nd Goums)

4th Group of Moroccan Tabors (Colonels Gautier and Parlange)
- Headquarters and Service Goum
- 5th Tabor (Headquarters, 41st, 70th, 71st Goums)
- 8th Tabor (Headquarters, 78th, 79th, 80th Goums)
- 11th Tabor (Headquarters, 88th, 89th, 93rd Goums)

APPENDIX III

Le Chant des Tabors

Drapeau unique des Goums Marocains
MAROC 1908–1934. TUNISIE 1942–1943. SICILE 1943.
CORSE 1943. ITALIE 1944. FRANCE 1944–1945.
ALLEMAGNE 1945. INDOCHINE 1948–1954.

Décoré de la Croix de la Légion d'Honneur en 1952.
de la Croix de Guerre 1939–1945 avec 1 palme.
du Mérite Militaire Chérifien.

LE CHANT DES TABORS

Refrain:

Regardez les Goums qui passent, l'oeil brûlant comme des loups.
Quoi qu'on dise, ou quoi qu'on fasse, il faut bien compter sur nous
Annibal et sa légende ne sont plus qu'un bruit très lointain.
Nous avons promené nos bandes, de l'Atlas, par-delà le Rhin.
Dans les rangs des G.T.M., à l'appel du grand AUROCH,
Retentit "Zidou l'goudem!" Pour la France! Pour le Maroc!

Zidou l'goudem, Zidou l'goudem
Ecoutez le Chant des Tabors
Marchez toujours, marchez quand même
Jusqu'à la fin, jusqu'à la mort
Tout en burlant "Zidou l'goudem!"
C'était la dure loi du Tabor.

Vêtus de nos robes de lame
Nous avons laissé nos troupeaux
Notre montagne ou notre plaine
Pour ne connaître qu'un drapeau
C'est le fanion d'un capitaine
Notre destin est le plus beau.

Rappelle-toi la Tunisie
Au temps de nos premiers assauts.
Rappelle-toi la frénésie
Qui s'empara de notre peau
Lorsqu'au Zaghouan—adieu la vie
Nous nous batîmes au couteau.

Sur le sol de la voie Appienne
Nous avons traîné nos pieds nus
Puis ce fut la course, vers Sienne
L'ennemi fuyait éperdu
Des baisers des belles Romaines,
Petit Goumier, te souviens-tu?

Le beau 15 août, ce fut la France
Qui nous reçut, les bras tendus
Nous apportant la récompense
Du bonbeur enfin revenu.
Marseille et toure la Provence
Ont chanté quand ils nous ont vu.

Coureurs de bled, coureurs d'espace
Bien serrés dans nos djellabas,
Il fallut poursuivre la chasse
Pendant l'hiver. O sombres mois!
Mais nous entrâmes en Alsace
Teintant de rouge le verglas.

Après le Rhin, la Forêt Noire
Nous vit surgir tels des démons.
On se ruait vers la victoire,

Par un soir d'avril nous plantions
Ah! le beau soir d'or de gioire
Dans le Danube nos fanions.

On chantera, la chose est sûre,
Pendant 100 ans et beaucoup plus,
Les exploits et les aventures
De ceux qui se sont tant battus.
Goumier, à la robe de bure,
Tu peux rentrer dans ta tribu.

Notes

CHAPTER 1

1. French Army Historical Service (Service historique de l'Armée de terre).
2. See William A. Hoisington Jr., *Lyautey and the French Conquest of Morocco,* for a detailed view of French political and military operations from 1902 to 1926, with emphasis on the contribution of Lyautey.
3. See A. Guillaume, *Les Berbères Marocaines et la Pacification de l'Atlas Centrale.* This is a very complete appreciation of the military side of the pacification, with an Order of Battle of the French units involved in each engagement and a French officer's view of the Berbers' fighting qualities.
4. Ibid.
5. For more on Berber language and customs, see Ernest Gellner, "Berbers of the Atlas" and David Seddon, "People of Morocco," both in *Peoples of the Earth.*
6. The Goumiers' superb fieldcraft was discussed in conversations with John Ryan who, while serving with the U.S. 9th Division in Sicily in 1943, was liaison officer to the 4th Moroccan Tabor. He recalls Goumiers pointing out German positions they could see with the naked eye that Ryan could barely discern through field glasses.
7. Mangin was better known for his later exploits as commander of the French 10th Army on the battlefields of World War I, where he was known as "the Butcher" for his somewhat reckless use of his own troops. See Barrie Pitt, *1918: The Last Act.*

8. French Army Historical Service.
9. Hoisington, *Lyautey and the French Conquest of Morocco.*
10. Ibid.
11. An interesting account of Klem's activities can be found in Charles Mercer, *Legion of Strangers.* See also Hugh McCleave, *The Damned Die Hard,* and Howard Swiggert, *March or Die.* All are colorful histories of the French Foreign Legion.
12. For road building in Morocco by the Legion, see Mercer, McLeave and Swiggert, ibid.
13. A general's eye view of this last campaign can be found in G. Ward Price, *Giraud and the African Scene.* Also Guillaume, *Les Berbers Marocaines.*
14. French Army Historical Service.
15. Ibid.
16. When later accused of being a collaborator, Noguès refuted this by saying, "I succeeded in concealing from them [the Germans] much of the more modern armaments belonging to the French Army. My 30,000 goumiers were all the time doing maneuvers with forbidden arms, but the Germans never found out." See Price, *Giraud and the African Scene.* For a less sympathetic view of Noguès see Ladislas Farago, *Patton: Ordeal and Triumph.*
17. See William B. Breuer, *Operation Torch,* for details of the Allied landings in North Africa. The Goums were not officially involved in these operations, but apparently their reputation had already reached the ears of the Americans. Breuer reports: "the men of Company G, 30th Infantry, were peering through the blackness at an outpost near Fedala [Morocco]. It was 2 A.M. on November 11th. The G.I.s were especially alert. They had heard a rumor earlier in the night that a small force of Berbers, fierce warriors from the mountains of Morocco feared for their skill with long, razor-sharp knives, had infiltrated American positions, silently hacked up four soldiers, and melted into the night."

18. See Dan Kurzman, *The Race for Rome.*

CHAPTER 2

1. Another such story, later reported in the Time-Life Books series "World War II," concerned the French officer who asked a Goumier going out on patrol to bring him back a German wrist watch. The Goumier returned with a bloody bag containing the prize—still attached to the severed arm of its original owner.
2. Derrien remained in Tunisia and was tried by a special French tribunal in March 1944. He was dismissed from the navy and sentenced to life imprisonment, but was released in 1946 and died shortly thereafter. See Martin Blumenson, *Kasserine Pass.*
3. Eddy Bauer, *Illustrated World War II Encyclopedia.*
4. Perhaps a better description is given by C. Ward Price in *Giraud and the African Scene* when he pictures the Dorsales as "being in the shape of a forked radish."
5. Blumenson, *Kasserine Pass.*
6. The Eighth Army fought its way up the coast as far as Enfidaville and then turned inland where it was stopped at Djebel Garci. It was then decided to abandon the push inland and proceed northward along the Mediterranean shore. In the final battles Anderson's First Army had the leading role over Montgomery's Eighth.
7. For a detailed account of the French XIX Corps' activities, see General Louis-Marie Koeltz, *Une campagne que nous avons gagnée: Tunisie 1942–1943.*" (A campaign that we have won: Tunisia 1942–1943).
8. De Monsabert later commanded the famed 3rd Algerian Division in the fight for Rome and the invasion of southern France and then led a corps of the French First Army in the fighting in France and Germany. See Lieutenant-Colonel Chester V. Starr, ed., *From Salerno to the Alps—A*

History of the Fifth Army, 1943–1945, and General Jean de Lattre de Tassigny, *History of the First French Army.*

9. See Koeltz, *Une campagne que nous avons gagnée.*
10. See George F. Howe, *Northwest Africa: Seizing the Initiative in the West.*
11. For the prewar North African adventures of General Giraud see Price, *Giraud and the African Scene*, and Guillaume, *Les Berberès Marocaines et la pacification de l'Atlas Centrale* (The Moroccan Berbers and the pacification of the Central Atlas).
12. See Lieutenant-General Omar N. Bradley, *A General's Life.*
13. See Lieutenant-General Sir Brian Horrocks, *Escape to Action.*
14. "Captain" may seem a very junior rank for a battalion commander, but at that time the administration of the French army was in disarray and promotion was slow and plagued by red tape. Anyway, judging from results, Verlet did a good job.
15. For dissident views on Sicilian Campaign strategy and tactics see Bradley, *A General's Life*; Carlo d'Este, *Patton: A Genius for War*; Ladislas Farago, *Patton: Ordeal and Triumph*; Hanson W. Baldwin, *Battles Lost and Won*; and W. G. F. Jackson, *The Battle for Italy.*
16. Elements of Keyes' Provisional Corps entered Palermo to the cheers of the populace on July 22, and Patton later established himself in a royal palace. Ibid.
17. At this stage of the war cooperation between air and ground forces was not good, and throughout the Tunisian and Sicilian campaigns instances of "friendly fire" were all too frequent.
18. "The Big Red One" had taken heavy casualties at Troina and was in a bad state. It was at this point that Bradley relieved both the division commander, Major-General Terry Allen and the assistant division commander, Brigadier-General Theodore Roosevelt Jr. Both men served with great distinction later in the war. See Bradley, *A General's Life.*

19. An exception was made in Baldwin, *Battles Lost And Won,* where the Goumiers of the 4th Moroccan Tabor are described as "of considerable psychological but little military importance" in the Sicilian Campaign. The author goes on to record that: "About 900 Berber goumiers, tribesmen with a liking for cold steel and a bloodthirsty reputation for toughness, night fighting and throat-slitting, fought in Sicily under French officers and non-coms, with 117 horses and 126 mules as their supply train."
20. This insignia can be seen exhibited in the *Musée de l'Armée* in Paris, along with uniform items and other Goumier artifacts.
21. Because the maquis-covered Corsican countryside had been long used as a hiding place for bandits and rebels, the term "maquis" became a nickname for the Resistance throughout France in World War II.
22. After the fighting ceased, a bronze plaque was placed along the road into Bastia in memory of the Goumiers of the 2nd GTM who had died in the battles there.

CHAPTER 3

1. Chester G. Starr, ed., *From Salerno to the Alps—A History of the Fifth Army, 1943–1945.*
2. French Army Historical Service.
3. Charles DeGaulle, *War Memoirs.* Vol. 2, *Unity.*
4. French Army Historical Service.
5. Mark W. Clark, *Calculated Risk.*
6. The author first heard this story in North Africa in 1943 from a British officer, who told it about the Gurkhas.
7. French Army Historical Service.
8. An advance of ten miles. W. G. F. Jackson, *The Battle for Italy.*
9. G. Ward Price, *Giraud and the African Scene.*
10. French Army Historical Service.
11. Dan Kurzman, *The Race for Rome.*

12. Starr, *From Salerno to the Alps.* The German Air Force Field Divisions were troops formed from excess personnel of the Luftwaffe, which had been decreasing rapidly in size and effectiveness. While some of these made good infantrymen, others did not.
13. Jackson, *The Battle for Italy.* De Gaulle's *War Memoirs,* however, puts the POW bag at 2,300.
14. Personal recollection. The author recalls seeing the Senegalese troops marching through Bastia on their return from Elba loaded down with household goods, pots and pans, livestock, all sorts of loot. Also French Army Historical Service.
15. Starr, *From Salerno to the Alps.*
16. Kurzman, *The Race for Rome.*
17. Clark, *Calculated Risk.*
18. Starr, *From Salerno to the Alps.*
19. Fred Majdalany, *Cassino: Portrait of a Battle.*
20. French Army Historical Service.
21. Ibid.

CHAPTER 4

1. Jean de Lattre de Tassigny, *History of the First French Army.* This important volume is a principal source of information, in English, for the French campaigns in France and Germany in 1944–45.
2. Brigadier Peter Young, ed., *World Almanac Book of World War II.*
3. Eddy Bauer, *Illustrated World War II Encyclopedia.* For an overall picture of the landings in southern France see Jeffery J. Clark and Robert Ross Smith, *Riviera to the Rhine,* and William B. Breuer, *Operation Dragoon.*
4. The 69th Algerian Artillery Regiment was chosen for this task. It had supported the Goums in Italy and would continue to do so throughout the French campaigns.

5. De Lattre, *History of the First French Army.*
6. French Army Historical Service.
7. Charles E. Pfannes and Victor A. Salamone, *The Great Commanders of World War II,* Vol. III.
8. De Gaulle, *Memoirs,* Vol. II.
9. French Army Historical Service.
10. De Lattre, *History of the First French Army.*
11. Jacques Augarde, *Tabor.* This small volume reveals many sidelights on life in the Goums by a lieutenant in the 1st GTM.
12. Pierre Lyautey, *La Campagne de France.* An historical account with personal views by an officer of the Goums.
13. With neither adequate bridging equipment nor sufficient boats and with the enemy still on all sides, a crossing would have been impossible anyway. At this time and place it was no more than a dream.
14. The Goumiers were on their good behavior in France. If there were any instances of serious malfeasance, they were not made public.
15. Clark and Smith, *Riviera to the Rhine.*
16. A bizarre sidelight of the fighting was a futile defense of the Colmar fortress by a "deaf battalion" of German soldiers. While most of the men of this unit were simply hard of hearing, some of the officers were in more serious condition with rheumatism, sciatica and even heart trouble.
17. This was the last battle of the 3rd GTM in France. Its long-planned relief took place on February 2, 1945, when it quit the front to return to North Africa. It was replaced in March by the 4th GTM.

CHAPTER 5

1. See Charles de Gaulle, *Memoirs*; de Lattre, *History of the First French Army*; and Charles B. MacDonald, *The Last Offensive.*

2. De Lattre, *History of the First French Army.*
3. Information supplied by a German resident of wartime Karlsruhe, now living in Canada.
4. MacDonald, *The Last Offensive.*
5. De Lattre, *History of the First French Army.*
6. MacDonald, *The Last Offensive.*

CHAPTER 6

1. Dan Kurzman, *The Race for Rome.*
2. John Ellis, *Cassino: The Hollow Victory.*
3. French Army Historical Service.
4. Ellis, *Cassino.*
5. *Chleuh* was, strictly speaking, the name given to the southern tribes of Morocco, but was commonly used for Moroccans in general as well as for the Berber dialects. *Chleuh,* the language, was often used in the tabors' radio transmissions to confuse the enemy.
6. Jacques Augarde, *Tabor.*
7. French Army Historical Service.
8. De Lattre, *History of the First French Army.*
9. Ellis, *Cassino.*
10. Lyautey, *Camets d'un Goumier.*
11. Ibid.
12. Ibid.

EPILOGUE

1. Europa Publications, *The Middle East and North Africa,* 19th edition.
2. See Alistair Home, *A Savage War of Peace.*
3. See Lucien Bodard, *The Quicksand War.* Godard obviously doesn't think much of the Tabors, citing the panic of the Moroccans at the culmination of the retreat from Cao Bang. On the other hand he specifically admires the 3rd Tabor of Commandant de Chergé.

4. For the full story of Dien Bien Phu see Bernard B. Fall, *Hell in a Very Small Place.*
5. The concept was based on that of the "Chindits," the British Long Range Penetration Groups that operated behind the Japanese lines in Burma in World War II. It was not very successful then, and it didn't work for the French in Indochina either.
6. Langlais, in command of all the parachute units at Dien Bien Phu, was a true *Africain,* having begun his military career as an officer of the *Compagnies Sahariennes,* the camel corps of Arab soldiers that policed the more remote parts of the Algerian Sahara in the heyday of the French Empire.
7. "Ardeche" was an area of France known for its deep valleys.
8. See Michael K. Clark, *Algeria in Turmoil.*

Glossary

Bled	French army term for the remote countryside
CC	Combat Command, an independent unit within an armored division, designated in American units as CCA, CCB and CCR (Reserve), and in French units as CC1, CC2 and CC3
DB	Division Blindée, French Armored Division
DFL	Division Frarwaise Libre, Free French Division
DIA	Division d'Infanterie Algérienne, Algerian Infantry Division
DIC	Division d'Infanterie Coloniale, Colonial Infantry Division
DIM	Division d'Infanterie Marocaine, Moroccan Infantry Division
DIMNI	Division d'Infanterie Marocaine de Montagne, Moroccan Mountain Division
FEC	French Expeditionary Corps
FFI	Force Frarwais d'Interieur, the French resistance movement
Goum	Company size unit of irregular Moroccan troops
Goumier	Individual member of a Goum
Groupe	Regimental size unit of irregular Moroccan troops
GTM	Groupe de Tabors Marocains, Group of Moroccan Tabors
Rezza	Moroccan version of the turban, wound from long strands of wool

RSA	Regiment de Spahis Algériens, Algerian Armored Regiment
RSAR	Regiment de Spahis Algériens de Reconnaissance, Algerian Reconnaissance Regiment
RTA	Regiment de Tirailleurs Algériens, Algerian Infantry Regiment
RTM	Regiment de Tirailleurs Marocains, Moroccan Infantry Regiment
RTS	Regiment de Tirailleurs Senegalais, West African Infantry Regiment
RTT	Regiment de Tirailleurs Tunisiens, Tunisian Infantry Regiment
Spahi	Regular North African cavalryman
Supplétif	Auxiliary soldier
Tabor	Battalion size unit of irregular Moroccan troops
Tirailleur	Regular North African infantryman
TM	Tabor Marocain, Moroccan Tabor
Zidou l'Goudem	Goumiers' battle cry, "Forward the Goums!"

Bibliography

Adleman, Robert H. and George Walton. *Rome Fell Today.* New York: Doubleday, 1975.

Al Shahi, Ahmed, ed. *People of the Earth.* Vol. 17. Danbury, Conn.: Danbury Press, 1933.

Augarde, Jacques. *Tabor.* Paris: France-Empire, 1952.

Baldwin, Hanson W. *Battles Lost and Won.* New York: Harper's, 1966.

Bauer, Eddy. *Illustrated World War II Encyclopedia.* Westport, Conn.: H. H. Stutunan, 1978.

Blumenson, Martin. *Kasserine Pass.* Boston: Houghton Mifflin, 1967.

Bodard, Lucien. *The Quicksand War.* Boston: Little, Brown, 1967.

Bradley, Omar N. *A General's Life.* New York: Simon and Schuster, 1983.

Breuer, William B. *Operation Torch.* New York: St. Martin's Press, 1985.

———. *Operation Dragoon.* Novato, Calif.: Presidio Press, 1987.

Clark, Jeffery J., and Robert Ross Smith. *Riviera to the Rhine.* Washington, D.C.: Center of Military History, U.S. Army, 1993.

Clark, Mark W. *Calculated Risk.* New York: Harper's, 1950.

Clark, Michael K. *Algeria in Turmoil.* New York: Grosset and Dunlap, 1950.

De Gaulle, Charles. *War Memoirs.* Vol. 2, *Unity.* New York: Simon and Schuster, 1959.

De Lattre de Tassigny, Jean. *History of the First French Army.* London: Allen and Unwin, 1952.
D'Este, Carlo. *Patton: A Genius for War.* New York: HarperCollins, 1995.
Ellis, John. *Cassino: The Hollow Victory.* New York: McGraw-Hill, 1984.
Europa Publications. *The Middle East and North Africa.* 19th ed. London: Europa Publications, 1972.
Fall, Bernard B. *Hell in a Very Small Place.* Philadelphia: Lippincott, 1966.
Farago, Ladislas. *Patton: Ordeal and Triumph.* New York: Ivan Obolensky, 1963.
Graham, Dominick, and Shelford Bidwell. *Tug of War: The Battle for Italy.* New York: St. Martin's Press, 1986.
Guillaume, A. *Les Berbères Marocaines et la pacification de l'Atlas Centrale* (*The Moroccan Berbers and the pacification of the Central Atlas*). Paris: R. Juilliard, 1946.
Hoisington, William A., Jr. *Lyautey and the French Conquest of Morocco.* New York: St. Martin's Press, 1995.
Home, Alistair. *A Savage War of Peace.* New York: Penguin Books, 1987.
Horrocks, Brian. *Escape to Action.* New York: St. Martin's Press, 1960.
Howe, George F. *Northwest Africa: Seizing the Initiative in the West.* Washington, D.C.: Center of Military History, U.S. Army, 1991.
Jackson, W. G. F. *The Battle for Italy.* New York: Harper & Row, 1967.
Koeltz, Louis-Marie. *Une campagne que nous avon gagnée:Tunisie 1942–1943* (*A campaign that we have won: Tunisia 1942–1943*). Paris: Hachette, 1959.
Kurzman, Dan. *The Race for Rome.* New York: Pinnacle Books, 1977.
Lyautey, Pierre. *Camets d'un Goumier.* Paris: R. Juilliard, 1945.
———. *La Campagne de France.* Paris: Plon, 1946.

MacDonald, Charles B. *The Last Offensive.* Washington, D.C.: Center of Military History, U.S. Army, 1973.

Majdalany, Fred. *Cassino: Portrait of a Battle.* New York: Longmans, Green, 1957.

McLeave, Hugh. *The Damned Die Hard.* New York: Saturday Review Press, 1973.

Mercer, Charles. *Legion of Strangers.* New York: Pyramid Books, 1965.

Pfannes, Charles E., and Victor A. Salamone. *The Great Commanders of World War II,* Vol. III. New York: Kensington, 1981.

Pitt, Barrie. *1918: The Last Act.* New York: Ballantine Books, 1962.

Price, G. Ward. *Giraud and the African Scene.* New York: Macmillan, 1944.

Starr, Chester G., ed. *From Salerno to the Alps—A History of the Fifth Army, 1943–1945.* Washington, D.C.: Infantry Journal Press, 1948.

Swiggert, Howard. *March or Die.* New York: Putnam, 1953.

Young, Peter, ed. *World Almanac Book of World War II.* Englewood Cliffs, NJ.: Prentice-Hall, 1981.

Index

Page numbers in italics indicates illustrations.

Stackpole Military History Series

Real battles. Real soldiers. Real stories.

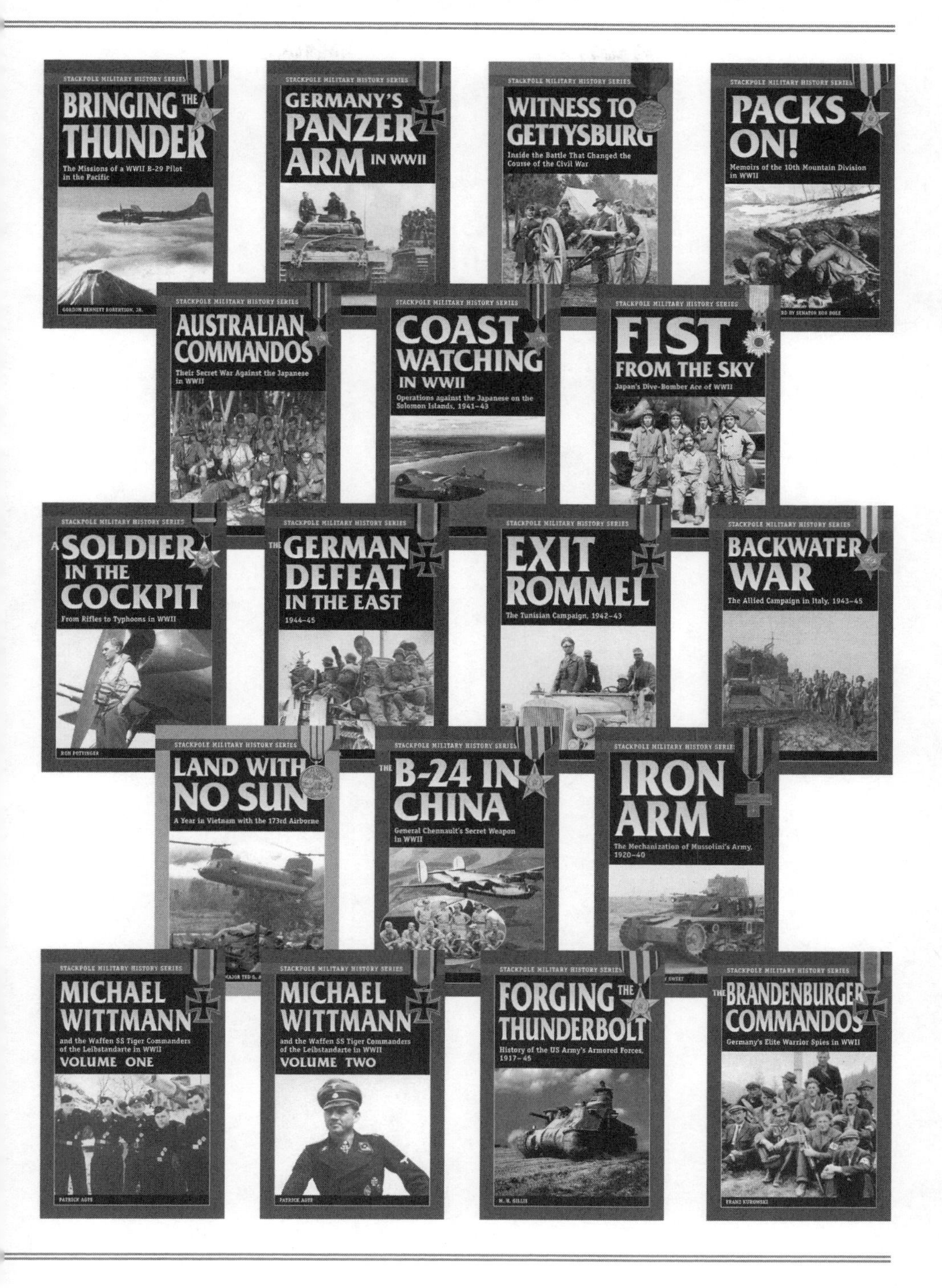

Stackpole Military History Series

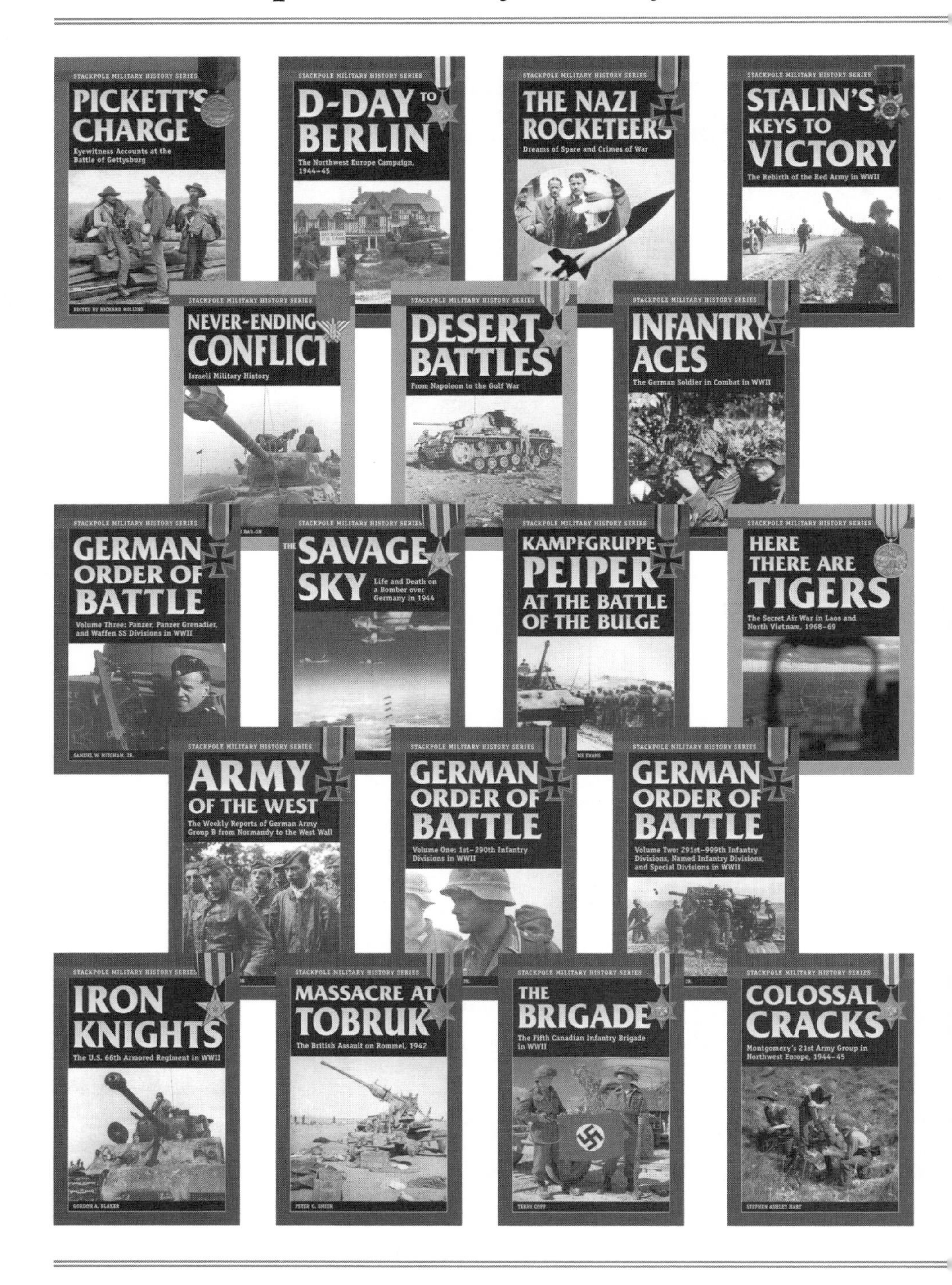

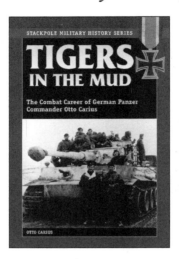

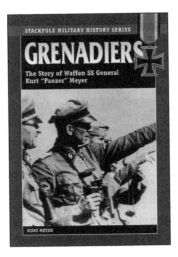

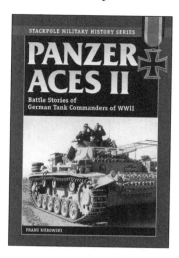

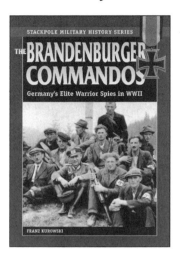

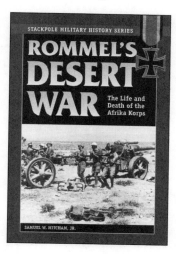

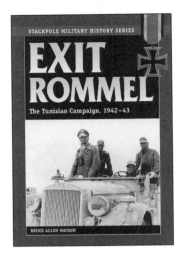

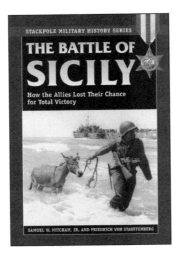

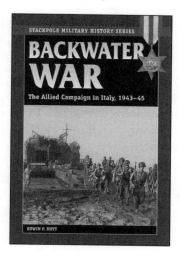

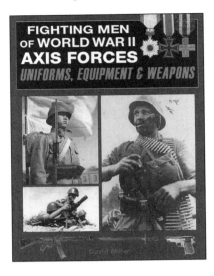